THE 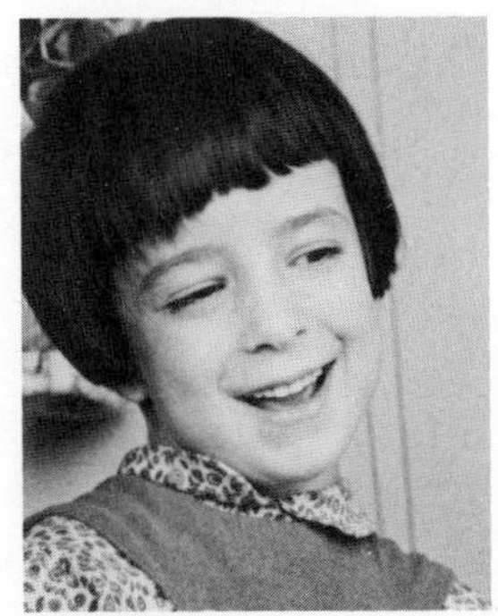 INNER 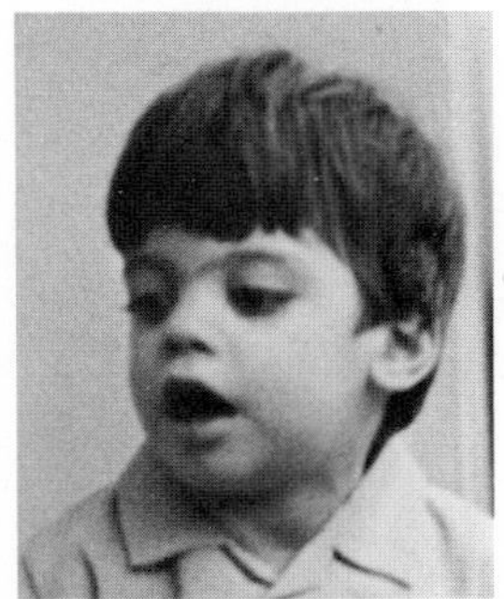

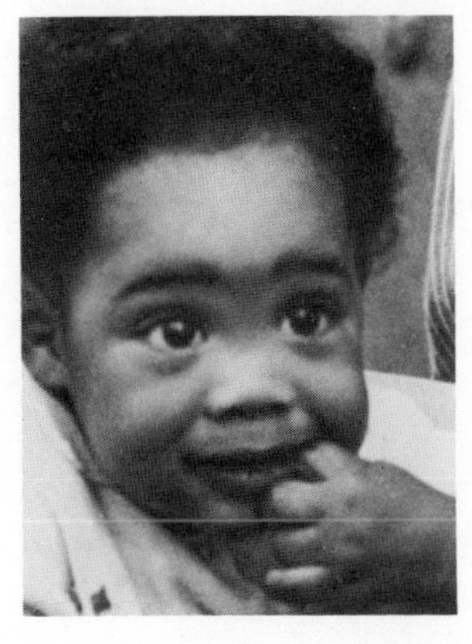 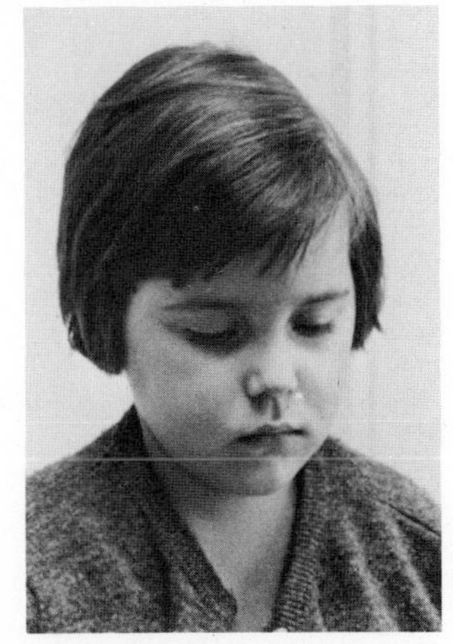

VOICES

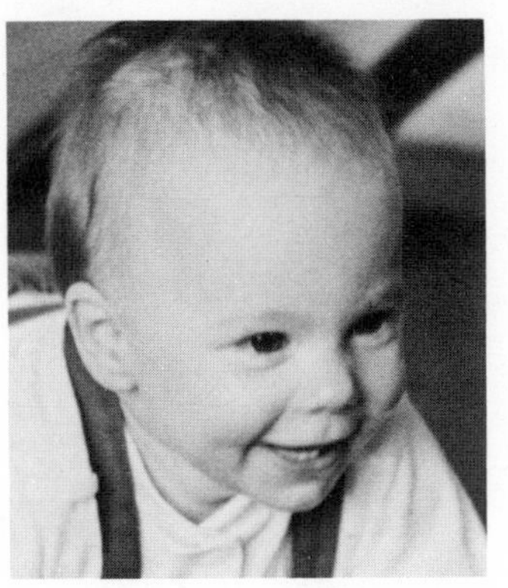

OF

CHILDREN

THE INNER VOICES OF CHILDREN

by J. LOUISE DESPERT, M.D.

Photographs by DUILIO PALLOTTELLI

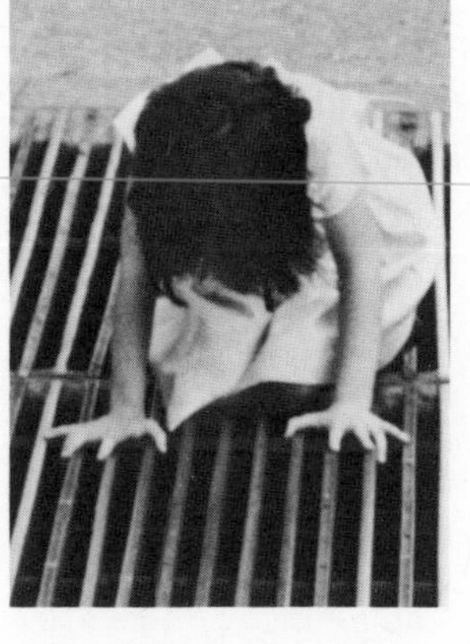

A FIRESIDE BOOK
PUBLISHED BY SIMON AND SCHUSTER

A Fireside Book
Published by Simon and Schuster
A Gulf+Western Company
Rockefeller Center, 630 Fifth Avenue
New York, New York 10020
Designed by Ella Mazel
Manufactured in the United States of America

1 2 3 4 5 6 7 8 9 10 Casebound

2 3 4 5 6 7 8 9 10 Paperback

Library of Congress Cataloging in Publication Data

Despert, Juliette Louise, 1892–
The inner voices of children.

1. Child Development. I. Title.
[DNLM: 1. Child behavior—Popular works.
2. Child development—Popular works. WS105 D468i]
HQ772.D48 1975b 155.4'13 75-44294

ISBN 0-671-22244-9
ISBN 0-671-22245-7 pbk.

Introduction

The author of this delightful book, a pioneer clinician in her field, needs no introduction to professionals in child psychiatry. Her contributions are as outstanding as they are numerous. This time, the eminent psychiatrist herself becomes a little child, regains the vision of the innocent eye, and gives verbal expression to the inner voices.

If there is one basic defect in the management of children, it is the failure to appreciate the fact that their world is not our world. This basic failure precludes any valid understanding of child life. What really matters is not what we do but rather how the child interprets what we do.

Amid a great deal of theoretical controversy, there is one bright area of consensus—the importance of infancy and early childhood in structuring the personality for better or for worse. The child is indeed father of the man. The nature of Man is locked in the secret of childhood. It is therefore particularly gratifying to welcome this book in which pivotal events in the development of all infants and young children are narrated in the child's own terms. The language is simple and clear and concise, as it tends to be when writers are in full command of their material.

Dr. Despert has succeeded admirably in selecting for her candid photographs the fleeting moments that vividly illustrate some of the stumbling blocks on the long road to maturity. From the first sequence of pictures on the "nursing adventure" through exploration, curiosity, toileting, sibling relationships, pain, and death, to the final scenes of family relationships, the reader is treated to an instructive and enjoyable harmony of superb text and illustrations. In the background, modestly hidden away, and emerging only at strategic intervals with a statement here and there, is the distinguished child psychiatrist, with her vast experience, her rare wisdom, and her permeating love of children.

It is my hope that the book will be widely read not only by parents experiencing the joys and responsibilities of guiding their children along the rocky road of the formative years, but also by the many workers in the away-from-home care of young children.

The book is deceptively simple; it merits careful reading and rereading.

Joseph H. Di Leo
Director of Developmental Clinic
New York Foundling Hospital

Preface

The minds of different generations are as impenetrable one by the other as are the monads of Leibniz.

ANDRÉ MAUROIS, *Ariel*

There is more to a child's behavior than meets the eye, a fact well known to perceptive mothers as well as to professional people involved with children—pediatricians, educators, psychiatrists, and psychologists. A child whose voice expresses surface compliance may be inwardly seething with anger. On the other hand, a loud, aggressive voice may represent an attempt to compensate for insecurity and anxiety.

Here is a child who is known to be generally happy; yet, even in the midst of engrossing play, there may pass over his face a shadow of deep concern, an anguish, fleeting but intense. Let us observe another child, idle, resting for a moment between active games. Is she really idle? Is her mind totally devoid of mental activity? Not likely. Although not as structured as those of adults, children's minds are ceaselessly occupied with fantasies they could hardly communicate if asked to do so at any particular instant. How do we know this? Children (as well as adults) may recall with great vividness early memories which they relive with an intensity of feeling that belongs to the early experience. Some of these experiences are verifiable as facts in the context of reality while others, vivid though they may be, are the recall of fantasies. Feodor Chaliapin, retracing his early years for

Maxim Gorky, expressed himself thus: "I made hideaways in the garden, built myself homes there, without parents, alone, free in the world. I dreamed of having my own farm and cattle. Vague, childlike dreams, and life was sometimes a fairy tale to me."

The inability to distinguish fantasy from reality is a normal stage in the development of young children. Only a few fail to go beyond this stage—needless to say, this is a serious deviation from normal behavior.

Gradually, the "normal" confusion disappears. This transition period is a difficult one for some parents who tend to see as "lying" what is only an immaturity in recognition. This is one of the two periods (the other is adolescence) rich in the inner life, productive of dreams and fantasies which the psychiatrist and psychologist make use of in their therapeutic approach. During these periods, the inner voices are denser, closer to the surface, more readily bursting through than at other times. In adolescence, the pressure may be so great that outbursts of deviant behavior, in various degrees of severity, may take place. This is a critical period for both parents and diagnosticians, as well as for the youngsters themselves, since the disturbance, which may be only transitory, often causes undue alarm. At such a time, the dialogue between parents and child is virtually nonexistent.

As audiovisual arts have become progressively more important in education and general communication, the dialogue within the family has been perceptibly reduced, when not completely annihilated. The compactness and closeness are not there. The interests of both parents and children are increasingly directed outward rather than inward.

Psychiatrists are familiar with children's inner worlds of fantasies, dreams, unconscious motives, and play projections. They deal with these every day as symbols to interpret in order to help children work out the internal conflicts which have made their lives miserable and unproductive, as well as contributed to the unhappiness of their families and others around them.

As a child psychiatrist, I have been preoccupied for many years with finding ways toward a better knowledge of the *inner* voices of children by correlating them with their *external* signs—not so much for professionals as for parents and other nonprofessional people. I felt that visual projections of what one might call critical points in emotional development would offer an opportunity to make such correlations. After a short period of trial and error, I was able to secure the collaboration of a gifted photographer whose training and experience in candid photography admirably suited my purpose. The pictures by Duilio Pallottelli were not shot randomly, nor were they limited to a rigid frame of reference. The suggestion was given him to be on the lookout not only for the specific, but also for the fortuitous. This dynamic, integrative process was the basis of THE INNER VOICES OF CHILDREN.

This is not a "How-to-do-it" book, nor does it attempt to illustrate all psychological phases of the child's emotional development. If it succeeds in stimulating an interest in what goes on "beneath the skin" in the life of the child, if it illuminates some behavior that may have seemed obscure at first glance, then the author and photographer will have been fully rewarded.

Contents

1. A baby is born 3
2. At first, the voices are somatic 9
3. Exploration, determination, and progress 15
4. No curiosity, no science 21
5. Leaving paradise behind 29
6. Cain started it—or did he? 33
7. Not so easy, this business of "when" and "where" 39
8. Maybe everybody, but not me 45
9. The grownups say "It's a great life," and that's what it is for real 51
10. The joy of eating 63
11. Just like Mommy, just like Daddy 67
12. Curiosity revisited 79
13. There are also the others 87
14. Discovering one's body 93
15. Why can't I have a pet? 97
16. Physical pain and body sensations 101
17. Parent-child associates 111
18. Even work can be fun 119
19. Where does the first step lead? 127
20. "Lost and found" 133
21. And some will show talent 139
22. Better not alone 145
23. Brothers and sisters 149
24. For the control of your body 153
25. No generation gap 157

Postscript 161

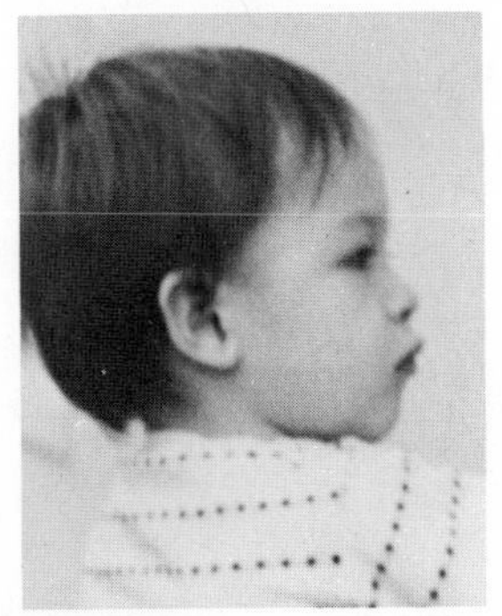

THE INNER

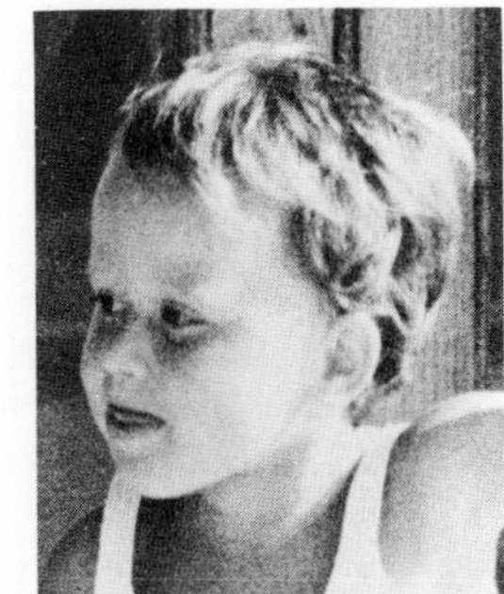

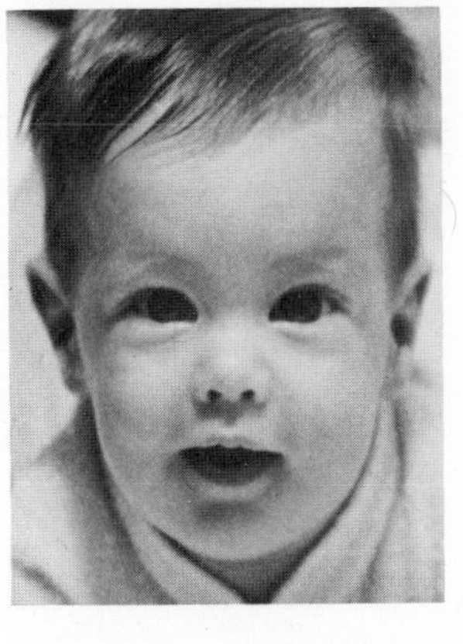

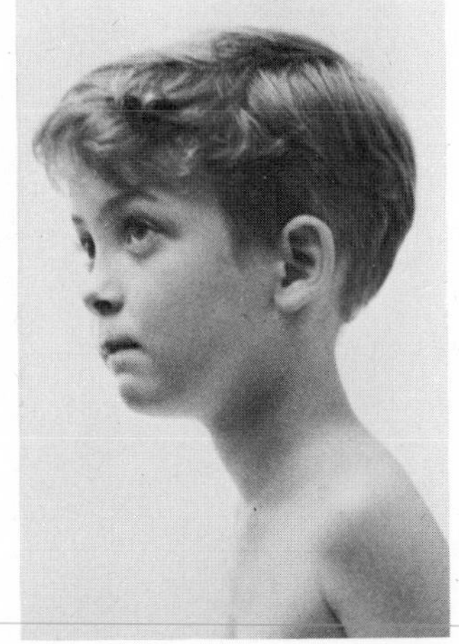

VOICES

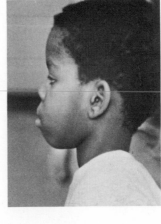

OF

CHILDREN

1

A baby is born

Lorsque l'enfant paraît, le cercle de famille
Applaudit à grands cris.

VICTOR HUGO

My mother groan'd! my father wept.
Into the dangerous world I leapt:
Helpless, naked, piping loud:
Like a fiend hid in a cloud.

WILLIAM BLAKE, *Songs of Experience*

A baby is born and, in most cases, it has a family circle to rejoice over its arrival. For nine months it has been growing from two microscopic cells conjugated into one to the complex, finished, though immature, independent human being that announces its entry into the world with a deafening howl. All out of proportion with the mass occupied, one may think. What is the meaning of this first cry? We know that it is necessary and that, if it is not immediately heard, the baby is "encouraged" to produce it by a firm slap on the buttocks. It is recognized that this vigorous crying causes the tiny air sacs (alveoli) of the lungs to open and thus initiate pulmonary breathing. The baby now depends on the unfolding of these air sacs to obtain the oxygen which in the womb was provided by the placenta from the mother's blood. No choice—it is either "get that oxygen or give up living outside your mother's body."

The cry has another meaning. Is it not a howl of protest? William Blake, as poets are wont to do, strikes the right note. Here is a very small being hidden from "the dangerous world," carefree, assured of adequate nourishment, moving weightlessly at even temperature in a fluid which buffers all shocks and vibrations—a shock absorber which also delivers the food. This small being now is released from its capsule, having contributed its share to the work of expulsion. It is released into an unfamiliar world, glaring with light, dry and comparatively cold without the protective coating of fluid. The mouth (freshly cleared of mucus) and the nose must both set to work pumping the air, a new and not so easy job.

Why should the newborn not protest? This cry can be considered the first "inner voice" loudly projected to the four corners of the baby's new world (PHOTOGRAPH 1). The "birth trauma," a concept formulated by Sigmund Freud and emphasized by Otto Rank, is here translated into unequivocal tones of anxiety. No words are available, nor are any necessary, to transmit the distress that grips the small baby ejected from its familiar, comfortable milieu. The birth anxiety is the prototype of all the anxieties, minimal to overwhelming, that any human being may experience in the course of a lifetime.

The newborn baby is helpless but has no way of knowing this; since all its needs are (for the majority of children) immediately satisfied, it cannot but acquire a sense of omnipotence—"ask and you get," and even, "before you can ask you get." This sense of omnipotence may stay past the stage of helplessness which has brought it on and justifies it; it may be encouraged to persist through overindulgence on the part of the parents and/or their desire to prolong the delightful "baby" state. Such infantilization is destructive; it stalls the healthy progression toward mature growth. We are all familiar with the type of child designated in common parlance as a "spoiled brat," a type well known to the psychologist, who calls such children overly "egocentric" (all young children are and have to be egocentric, but excesses hamper development). They are aggressive although deeply insecure, will not share any of their possessions, want their way always, make themselves insufferable to their group, in school or on the playground. Even though all their whims are satisfied and anticipated (in the family), they are not happy children—they whine, withdraw, and feel constantly frustrated. But this is anticipating.

The physical needs of babies are well recognized, and knowledge of these needs is now widely accepted and disseminated. Furthermore, babies have at their disposal a precious means of communication: their voices. If they are hungry, or made uncomfortable by cold air or wet diapers, a cry will immediately signal their need in easily deciphered messages.

What about their emotional needs? After a too-long period of "scientifically" prescribed detachment and aloofness ("Let the baby cry if he is well fed, warm and no pin is sticking him"), it is now recognized that children's emotional health hinges upon the early satisfaction of their hunger for maternal love. The physical closeness, the cuddling, the cooing—some of it a continuum from intra-uterine life—are imperative requirements. The research of two American psychiatrists, René Spitz and Margaret Ribble, leads to such explicit conclusions. The need for *mothering* is so well recognized that the modern foundling hospital, besides its carefully planned schedules for physical health, has in recent years added periods of mothering, generally provided by women volunteers since nurses seldom have the time for activities beyond feeding, diapering, and general watchfulness.

The progress achieved in the care of young children during the past half-century should not blind us to the truly awe-inspiring phenomenon of life in the womb. Children often ask me: "Do you believe in God?" To such a question there is no valid answer, except that usually provided by the family. It is not for

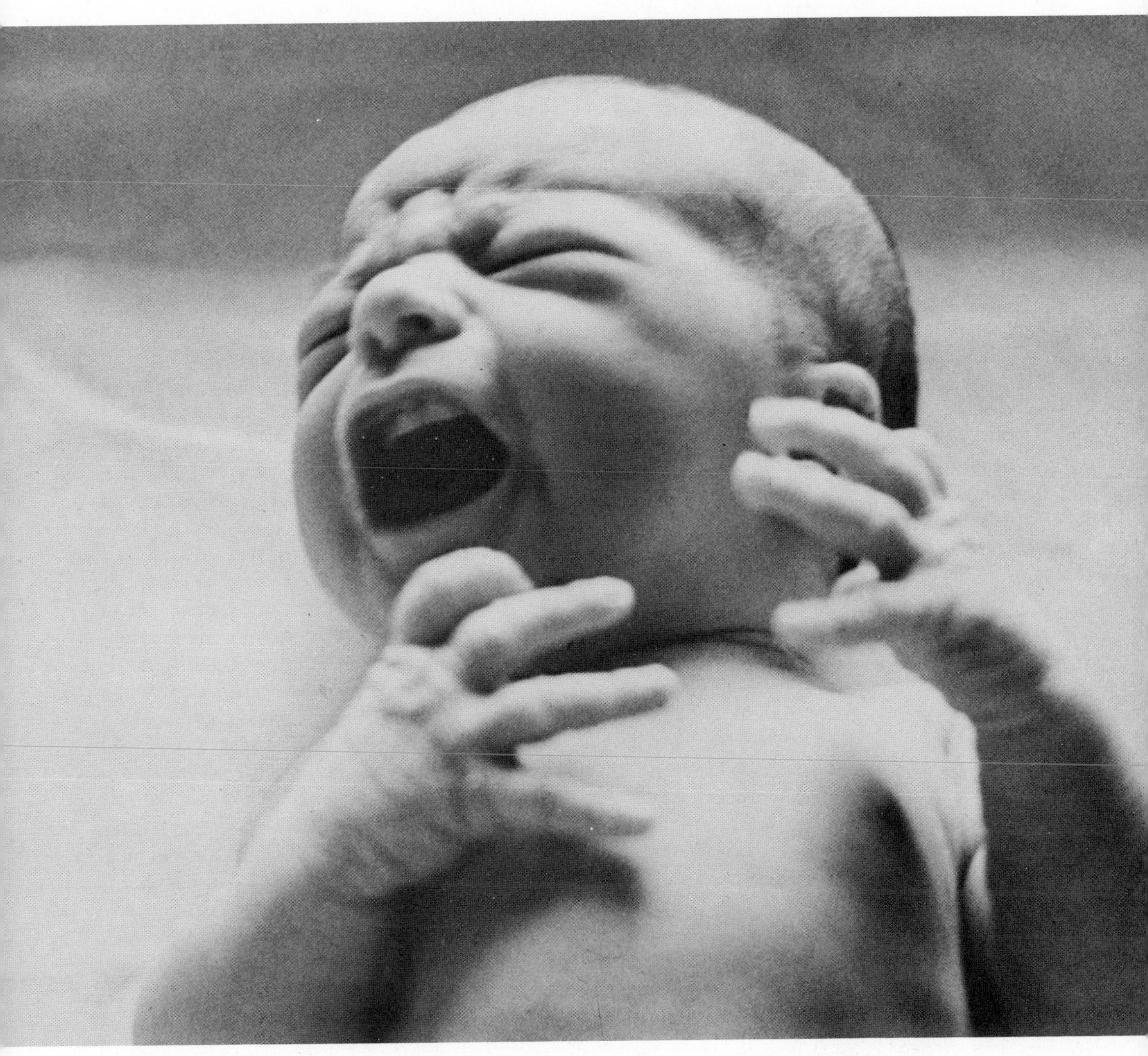

1

psychologists or teachers, whether they are agnostic or religious, to influence children with their own convictions. This I try to make clear. However, I find children ready to listen wide-eyed to the story of themselves before they were born. They already know they were growing in the mother's body. This is the first thing they have wanted to know: "Where did I come from?" How they got there is the next question, and this calls for more finesse in explaining the sexual union of the parents that resulted in their conception.

First there are two cells, so small they can't be seen except with a microscope (though not the kind they may have received as a birthday present, which is not powerful enough). The two cells join to form a single unique one, still microscopic in size. From this moment, following what must be a "Master Plan," this cell divides again and again. Billions of cells, diversified and already disciplined, group themselves into organs (a stomach, an eye, a kidney, and so on), each with its special job, never doing the job of another. Some cells are readying themselves to be used later (the retina in the back of the eye), some are already working at their job (the blood vessels transporting the blood). The cells of the gastric mucosa will only digest the foods, mostly proteins, that are processed in the stomach leading to their absorption in the blood, while the cells of the heart muscle will perform the various motor actions demanded of that capital organ. These, and many other operations, are under the command and participation of an intricate system of nerves and hormones.

The orchestration of all the various functions involved is so complex that it is impossible to describe it except in fragments—the specialization and synchronizations can hardly be comprehended in their total interaction. Indeed, scientists themselves can only study them in fragments. Man can add, remove, substitute, modify the parts, but is not able to create the whole. What is this force, this power, this Something that rings like a Master Mind, beyond and above man? I do not attempt to give a name to it, but I know from experience that children are able to respond to an evocation which, for all its lack of precision, arouses in them a feeling of immeasurable magnitude outside of themselves. In many instances, children spontaneously give it a name, and this name to them is God; but it matters not if the power remains nameless.

The newborn baby is a completed human being even though some systems are far from being fully developed. Look at PHOTOGRAPH 2, the picture of a baby boy taken a few hours after delivery. The hands are perfect miniature models of their adult counterparts. The facial features have a finished appearance. Nothing is missing or underdeveloped.

If anyone doubts the vigor and living power of this small being, it is not necessary to hear the yell of protest at birth (PHOTOGRAPH 1); one need only to study the mouth, widely open, almost distorted by the effort to produce that first inner voice, exploding.

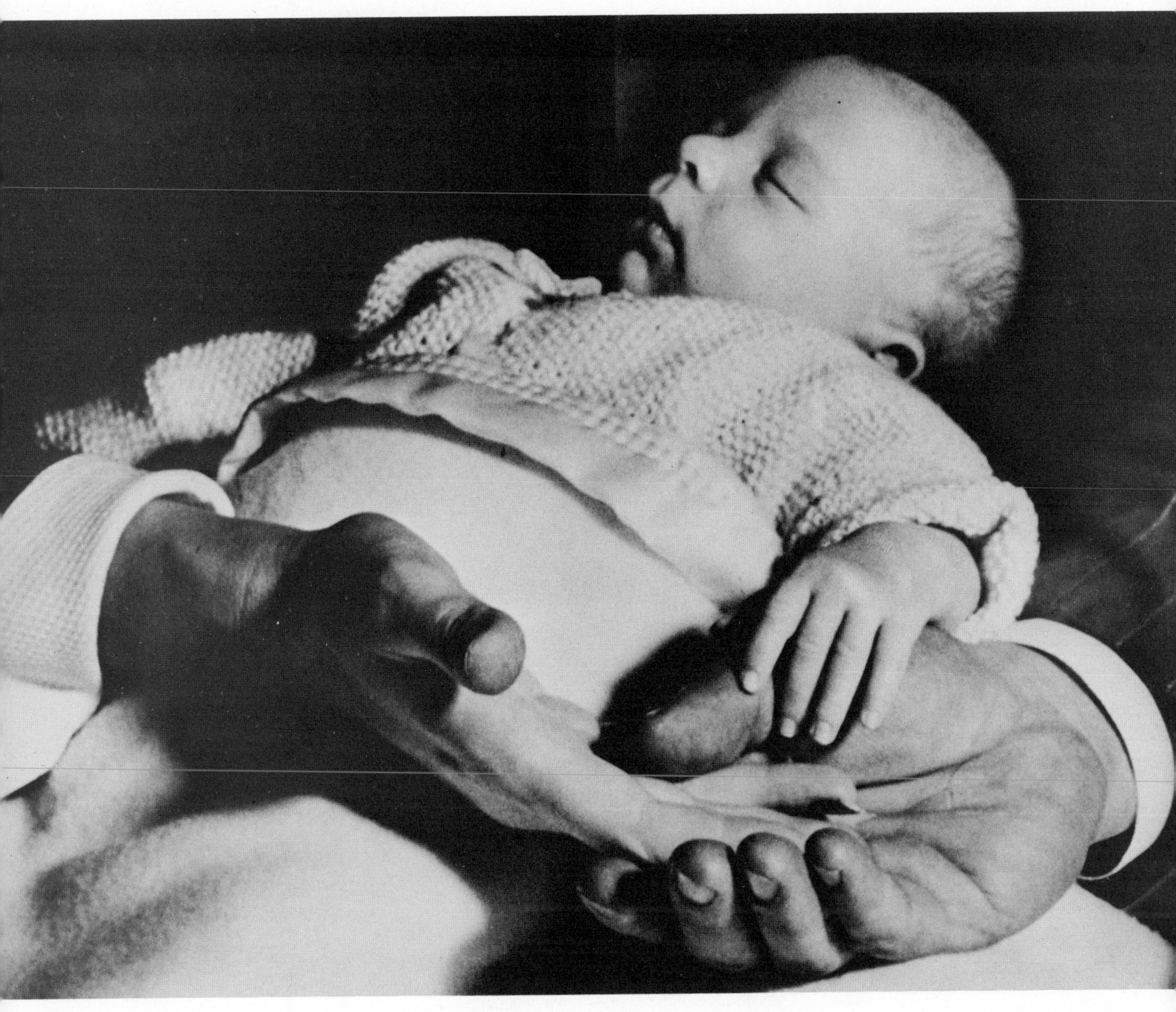

2

2

At first, the voices are somatic

> We must watch the infant in his mother's arms; we must see the first images which the external world casts upon the dark mirror of his mind, the first occurrence which he witnesses; we must hear the first words which awaken the sleeping powers of thought and stand by his earliest efforts if we would understand the prejudices, the habits and the passions which rule his life.
>
> ALEXIS DE TOCQUEVILLE, *Democracy in America*

At birth, the baby has only its voice to communicate its comforts and discomforts, pleasure and pain. Or so it seems. However, there are other channels of expression, all somatic, before the voice becomes expressive, and long before language has appeared. The whole body is involved in communication. Even at birth the protest and distress which are loudly voiced are accompanied by body movements, the meaning of which soon becomes explicit.

Because the central nervous system is immature and the nerve sheaths (myelin) are not fully developed until approximately the fifth year, the body movements are uncoordinated, awkward, "jerky." When the infant experiences pain or feels frustrated or wishes something (its feeding, for instance), it not only cries but becomes physically agitated, thrashes about with its whole body, its arms and legs engaged in movements which, compared to the controlled, coordinated, purposeful motor activity of the adult, seem out of proportion with the stimulus. These body expressions continue normally but to a lesser degree as auxiliaries to the vocal expression for several years. A two- or three-year-old who wants a toy on a high shelf, visible but not accessible, will not only ask for it, but will also move toward it, attempt to grasp

it. This is an automatic body move, and may be fraught with danger because of its impulsive character. An open window, a hot radiator, are no deterrents to the impulsive act.

Frustration expressed through body tensions is even more legible. PHOTOGRAPHS 3, 4, and 5 of four-week-old Victoria tell an eloquent story of awkward breast feeding as a source of frustration. They show a young mother, ill at ease with her first child in an unfamiliar situation, as evidenced in her rigid position, her maladroit gestures when offering her breast, and the way she holds her baby, who can only feel insecure and fear she might fall—her feet have no touching point and her body is close to her mother's body only partially in its upper part.

Victoria responds with marked body tension, her small body stiff as a rod. That she is frustrated is clearly seen in PHOTOGRAPHS 4 and 5, taken immediately after the feeding. The features are distorted, the body still rigid, and the facial expression is not that of a contentedly satiated breast-fed infant. Particularly revealing is that little left index finger in PHOTOGRAPH 5, which seems to point reproachfully to the source of her discomfort. The voices at this stage may be only somatic,

4

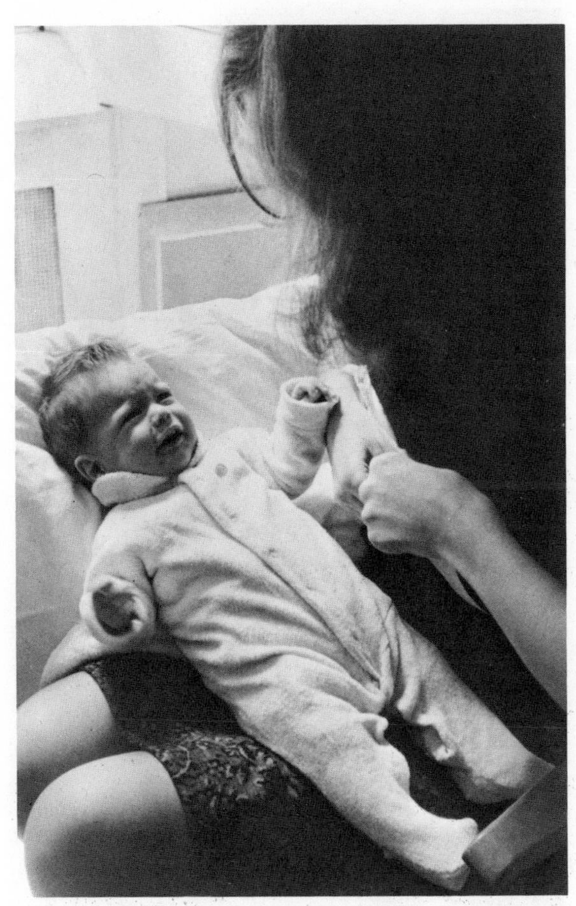

5

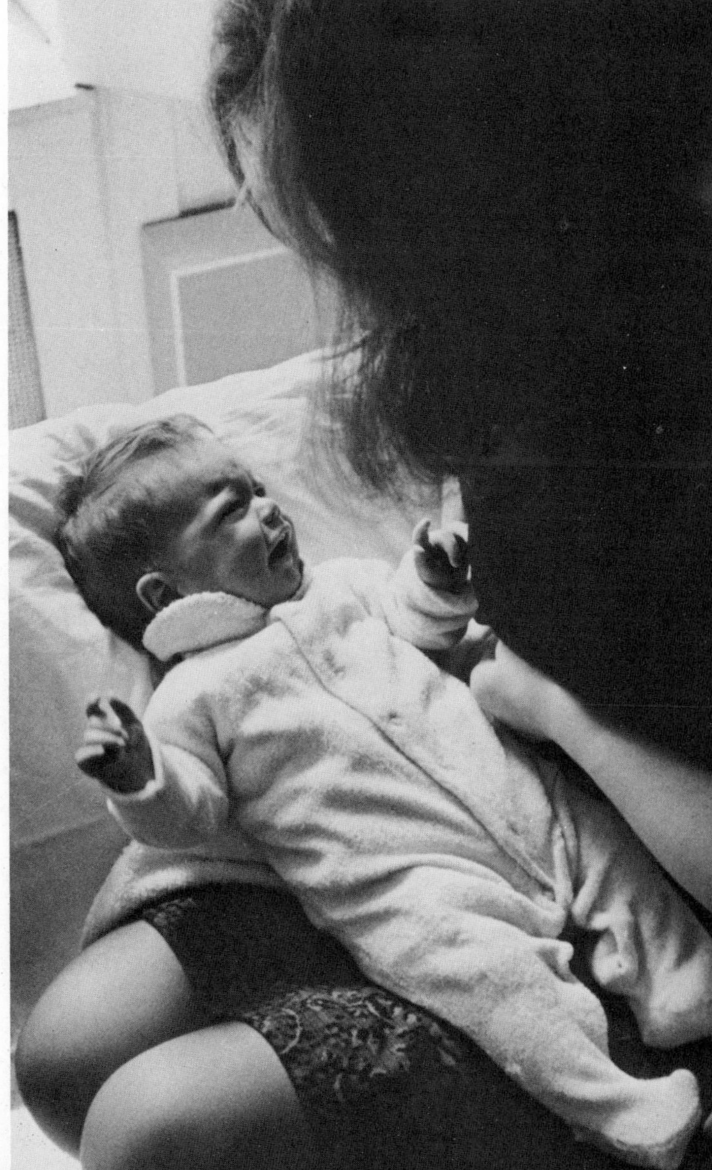

but can one deny their eloquence? No words, but a sad song to sing. Only a picture, but distressingly expressive.

A mother who has not wanted her baby, or who unconsciously rejects it, or who has been pressured to breast-feed it—such a mother would present a similar picture. In our case, none of these factors was operating. Although this young woman is known to be apprehensive and unprepared for her full role as a mother, there is no rejection here. But the baby has perceived a dissonance, to which she responds. It could be predicted that after a period of mutual exploration, willingness to try, to fail, to try again, the baby could at last find satisfaction in her mother's breast.

This is exactly what happened. In PHOTOGRAPHS 6, 7, and 8, of Victoria at two months, both mother and child are free of tension, the baby curling up in her mother's arms and at last enjoying the nursing adventure. A happy expression is registered on both faces, and the communication between parent and child is complete. No words are needed. In PHOTOGRAPH 8 she stares at her mother, and there can be no mistake about her several messages.

6

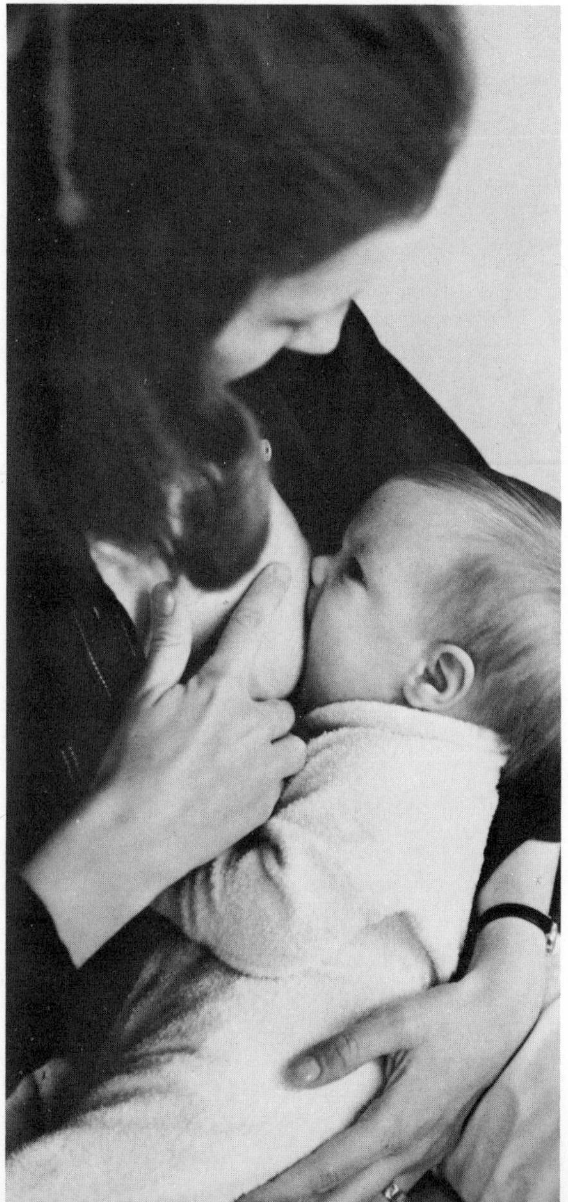

7

A baby does not voice only discontent or discomfort. Positive feelings are also registered, vocally and/or bodily. Intermittent sucking movements between feedings, sudden smiles or grimaces, muscular agitation, all correspond to some inner impulses which can only be partially identified. Dreaming in the early months cannot be proved, but it can be assumed. Animals, despite their limited mentation, are known to dream. A cat, for instance, seemingly in a deep sleep, can be observed to make abortive running movements accompanied by the special mouse-hunting cry which tells clearly that it is dreaming and reliving a mouse-catching experience. There follow masticatory motions and, so vivid has been the dream, after awakening the cat washes its mouth to remove all traces of its sumptuous repast.

To consider the baby's sucking while asleep only a reflex would be to ignore the beginning of the infant's inner life. The wish to repeat and relive a pleasurable experience, the smile that accompanies or immediately follows it, give us the picture of a dramatic sequence that surely goes beyond a pure reflex.

The infant's brain at birth is very immature. The experiences that would have made their stamp on the brain cells are extremely limited. It is not proven, but it can be assumed that, from birth, the infant's reactions to cold, excessive heat, hunger, its clamor and satisfaction, its responses to human contact (the mother's voice, cooing, handling), all, momentary though they be, leave an imprint which will be the basis of later evocations in the form of fantasies and dreams. A reservoir of images is thus steadily accruing and settling, mostly in the unconscious. These reemerge in their later forms as the foundations of early memories.

Working with neurotic and psychotic children, one is of necessity exploring recesses of the memory as far back as can be reached. How far back can actual memories be recaptured? Occasionally children will express the belief that a certain recalled experience occurred when they were a year old, before they were able to walk, for instance. Generally, verification is not possible. Was it a factual experience, or was it a fantasy? When did it appear? Seldom is it possible to "pin the evidence down." However, I recall a nine-year-old boy who came to treatment for a severe anxiety. As therapy proceeded, he was able to trace what seemed to be a fantasy, but which, he insisted, was something that had "really happened." He was sure that "it" had taken place when he was hardly one-and-a-half years old. He recalled many specific details with such vividness that I felt compelled to check on the facts with the parents: the layout of the room and its furniture, the design and color of the wallpaper. While the parents had not been witnesses to the traumatic experience recalled by the boy (involving him and his nurse), they confirmed that he could not have been more than eighteen months old because when he was that age the family had moved.

It is not always possible to obtain such precision about early memories and fantasies; the earlier they are, the more difficult is the recovery. Actually, from a therapeutic point of view it is not imperative that the distinction be made. The intensity of the affect associated with the memory (whether fact or fancy) is what counts most for the psychiatrist. What we are concerned with now is the beginning of the inner voices of children.

The baby is bombarded by impressions it receives through its senses. Some are pleasurable, some are not. Some leave an enduring imprint, others are evanescent. They all contribute to the building up of a fund of inner experiences which seek their way of expression. The impulse to communicate can be detected early, even before it is oriented and coordinated. What happens to the communication? It may be accepted, even greeted with glee, but it can also be censured. A message for a child to keep. *Grownups have ways of their own about what can and cannot be. One sees things, one hears things, one smells things that grownups say don't exist. Back to their hidden channels go these wonderful possessions, truly one's own. No grownup is going to dig them out unless one is willing to give them up.*

3

Exploration, determination, and progress

Yet all experience is an arch wherethrough
Gleams that untravelled world. . . .

ALFRED, LORD TENNYSON, *Ulysses*

Once the baby's back muscles have developed enough to permit the sitting position, the world takes on a new aspect. People and objects are seen from a different angle, not as remote and depersonalized as they were from the lying-down vantage point. This takes place from approximately six to nine months, a span whose length depends on many factors: heredity to begin with, then the environment, where babies are variously stimulated to reach, to grasp, and to touch with a whole gamut of pleasurable reactions. It will not be long before the mother will sit her baby on the pot, and if she has carefully noted the rhythm and pattern of defecation, and does not apply pressure, she may see the beginning of timing and, still later, control. She soon learns, or should learn, that no enticement or forcefulness will bring the desired results.

Being able to sit and having back muscles strong enough for certain performances announces a full range of new activities, crawling being foremost. For most babies, crawling precedes standing alone and walking. Some of them, well able to stand and walk, linger over crawling. Take one-year-old Curtis who, in PHOTOGRAPH 9, has walked toward his father's library. His glance goes over the many, many books on the shelves. *But who*

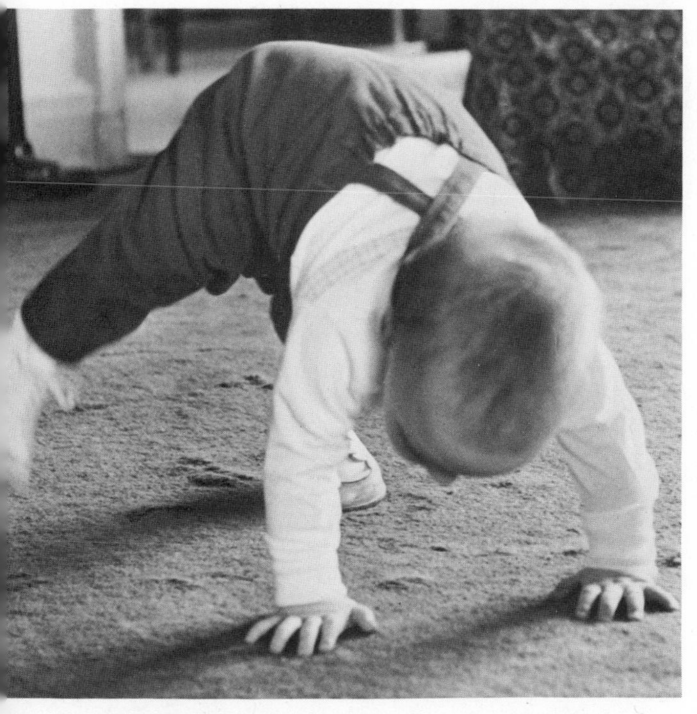

cares about books at his age except to pull them apart, take a taste of, or chew at them —not so pleasant, that. Besides, someone is always around to prevent you from even trying it. But crawling! How fast one can cover the whole room, hither and thither (PHOTOGRAPH 10)! The whole world is here, all around, the wastebasket with its intriguing scraps of paper that one can look at while holding on to the shoe tree that has proved of lasting interest (PHOTOGRAPH 11). At this age, the mouth, which has been since birth the center of sensations and contact with the outside world, still holds a dominant place. Curtis has not exhausted the endless pleasures such an exotic "toy" can offer: the taste, the texture, the feeling on the gums which are at present mildly painful with teeth coming through. Curtis knows nothing about dentition, congested gums, and gum

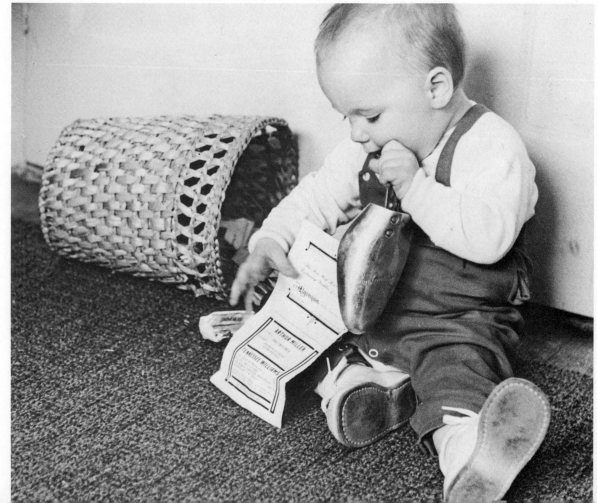

11

soothers, but he would defend his shoe tree against all intervention. Besides, this shoe tree is his father's.

Full speed ahead goes Curtis about all the accessible space, consenting to walk only for a brief demonstration of skill—or so one might assume. In the course of his exploratory travel on all fours, he has just sighted an unfamiliar object, the photographer's camera case. To get to it, investigate it, and if possible take possession of it, is next on the program. From the floor, it no doubt seems to our little globetrotter as high as the Himalayas, with a couch and a window sill to overcome on the way. Is this going to dampen Curtis's enthusiasm for the strange black object? Not in the least. Undaunted, he begins to climb, not too successfully at first. Flat on his face, he finds himself with no broader horizon than couch seat, and more couch seat (PHOTOGRAPH 12). An upward heave, and hope brightens: the left hand can almost reach the edge of the window sill. The determination to get there is reflected in the muscular tonus of that little body, tense, dedicated, and single-purposed (PHOTOGRAPH 13). At last, at last, the goal is reached. Note the authority with which that left hand asserts itself, fully spanned on the lid, and the complete domination of the pursued treasure by its pursuer (PHOTOGRAPH 14). In PHOTOGRAPH 15 he is in full control, and later he even succeeds in lifting the lid from the case.

The sequence illustrated here is the key to much of the behavior of the young child as a toddler. "He gets into everything," parents are prone to complain. Indeed this age is

12

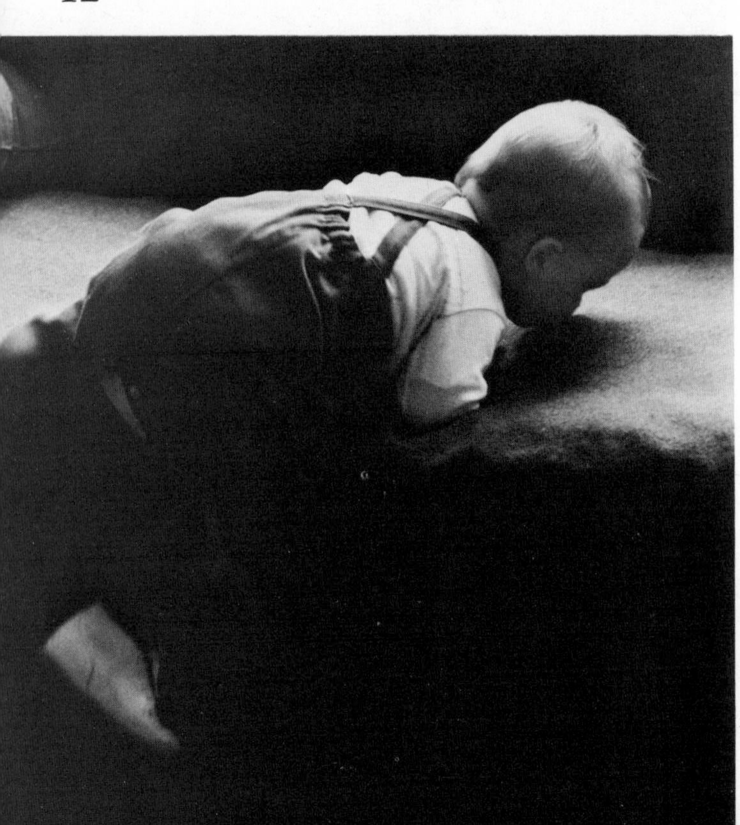

13

probably the one that makes the most demands on the adult in charge, who is torn between the wish to allow freedom of movement and the need to preclude dangerous adventures. Curtis is safe because there is always a parent or nurse with a discreet eye on him, ceaselessly monitoring, but also allowing the child to get around within limits dictated by the concern for his safety.

This is not the lot of all children: overpermissiveness and overdiscipline are two ap-

14

15

proaches widely divergent in nature which are nevertheless similarly destructive. Here is an incident I observed which shows how not to do it. Several years ago, I was driving along a wide and busy New York street; buses, trucks, and passenger cars were moving at varying speeds. Suddenly, about ten feet ahead of my car, a fifteen- to eighteen-month-old boy toddled out of the space between two parked cars on my right. I stopped the car and blew the horn frantically to alert other motorists, to call the attention of the person responsible for the child, and possibly to startle the child enough so that he would stand still. This is exactly what happened. The mother, absorbed in conversation with two other women, had lost contact with her child. Now she rushed to pick him up and, without a word, spanked him soundly.

Spanking is never recommended as a method of training. One can assume that the mother, upset and feeling guilty, did relieve her own tension through this irrational gesture. The child, however, could not grasp the meaning of the punishment. A minute or two must have elapsed since he had taken off from the sidewalk and nothing now could make him connect the two separate occurrences. Understandably, he screamed his anger. No lesson was learned. A child must be protected from his own recklessness and prevented from running into danger. There is plenty of time ahead for the enjoyment of freedom and unbridled self-expression. Our little adventurer had listened to the inner voice telling him how much more exciting was the street, with all those cars whizzing by with a whoosh and a vroom, than standing there near Mommy, her friends, and their monotonous drone.

Going back to Curtis—the reader will not have failed to note the intense delight pervading the round of activities that ended in the mastery of an almost impossible feat. That Curtis had an audience (the photographer, his father, and possibly others) only added to his enjoyment even if, absorbed in his game, he seemed to pay no attention to them. At his age, all children are hams. They like to perform for the benefit of an audience, apart from the excitement of achievement for its own sake. The psychologist calls this exhibitionism, a normal trait at this stage. If it persists, or reappears in adult life, it becomes pathological and can be fraught with devastating social consequences.

Another observation can be made concerning Curtis's short sequence of activities. While gravitating toward his goal, he is completely involved with the "task" at hand. His concentration is total; no outside stimulus could distract him from his self-imposed assignment. It cannot be said that Curtis is not "engagé." Mouth, hands, feet, are operating with maximum efficiency and intent. His nurse rightly says of him, "He is all mouth and hands," which is as it should be, for the drive to grasp, get, keep, and take to mouth is strongest at this age. The world is there, all around, for Curtis to incorporate, take to his mouth—actually to himself.

4

No curiosity, no science

> A child said *What is the grass?* fetching it to me with full hands . . .
>
> WALT WHITMAN, *Song of Myself*

Curiosity in the young child could justifiably be taken as a measure of intelligence, even though tests cannot be devised to give accurate measurements. Meticulous observation must suffice. Long before infants have acquired a vocabulary for the description of what they see, it is apparent that they have perceived a great deal of what surrounds them. They seem to be on the lookout for new perceptions. With what delight do they discover their fingers, their toes, first as independent objects, then as part of themselves.

When does curiosity—this looking for new configurations, movements, and objects—arise? This is difficult to ascertain. The fact that a baby fixes its attention on an object held in its field of vision does not necessarily prove that it is curious about this object. Granted that a response to sound is a reflex, an element is added to this reaction when a baby hears its mother's voice, turns to the direction the voice comes from, and maintains an expression of expectancy until the mother appears. It can be assumed that the baby recognized the voice and is curious about it.

Young children are quick to detect small defects or distortions—a greasy spot on a material, an electric switch that stands slightly awry, an infinity of details that go unnoticed by the adult eye. In the course of a project at the Payne Whitney Nursery School, children aged two to five were taken individually to a playroom three flights above the ground floor level of the school. Throughout the building, there was a call system for the doctors which operated through round devices about two inches in diameter, located in all rooms and corridors on the walls, close to the ceiling. The central hammer, one-quarter inch in diameter, tapped the number wanted. A four-year-old girl I had brought to the third floor called my attention to the tap device in the corridor, noting it was not the same as the one in the Nursery School though acknowledging that the sounds were the same. She was adamant—"No, downstairs is different"—when I insisted they were identical. She felt so strongly about it that I decided to check again, and sure enough there was a difference—barely perceptible—but a difference. When the walls of the corridor had been repainted recently, the minute hammer had been overlooked and it was a different color than the remainder of the device. This, six feet over the child's head.

I was so intrigued by the child's observation and her curiosity about it, that I asked several adults to look carefully at the tap device and tell me if they saw any difference between it and others in the building. They did not. Granted that adults must narrow their field of vision, that they can no longer afford to be randomly curious about their surroundings since they are focusing on whatever object is their concern at the moment—the fact of the curiosity and sharp perception of the child remains.

PHOTOGRAPH 16 shows a one-month-old baby who stirs from under his blanket and raises his head the better to see what is going on. And what indeed is going on? Simply that an unfamiliar person—the photographer—has invaded the privacy of his narrow, familiar world. *Who is this person? What is he doing here with the clicking, the flash of light? What is it all about?* He is straining so much to lift his head that transverse "wrinkles" have appeared on his forehead. He cannot maintain the body tension—his musculature is not developed enough—nor can he keep his eyes wide open for very long, but at this moment he takes in all he can.

Curiosity is characteristic of all ages of childhood. Before children are asked to apply their curiosity to prescribed subjects in school, they have filled their minds with observations of their own choice. Adults often get impatient with the flood of questions thrown at them by children who see a multitude of persons and objects and make little sense of their actions and confusing presence. They are curious not only about their surroundings but about what is "going on inside" themselves. Sometimes the two merge with cunning or disarming simplicity to torment you: *your shadow becomes a monster that will attack you, if not now then while you sleep; your little brother will drown in your dream.* They also merge to form delightful patterns of things to come: *maybe you could fly like Superman, arms out and a cape on the shoulders* (then you land ignominiously on the floor, having started from some high point—father's chest of drawers, for instance—but this you do not know yet and cannot, or refuse to, visualize); *you would drive an automobile so fast nobody could catch up with you.* The world is full of possibilities.

The curiosity of children is a delight to some parents, but it can be irritating to others. From the time they learn to speak until the age of five or six, they discover the magic words "What?" "Who?" "Why?" "When?" "How?" "Where?" These words invariably

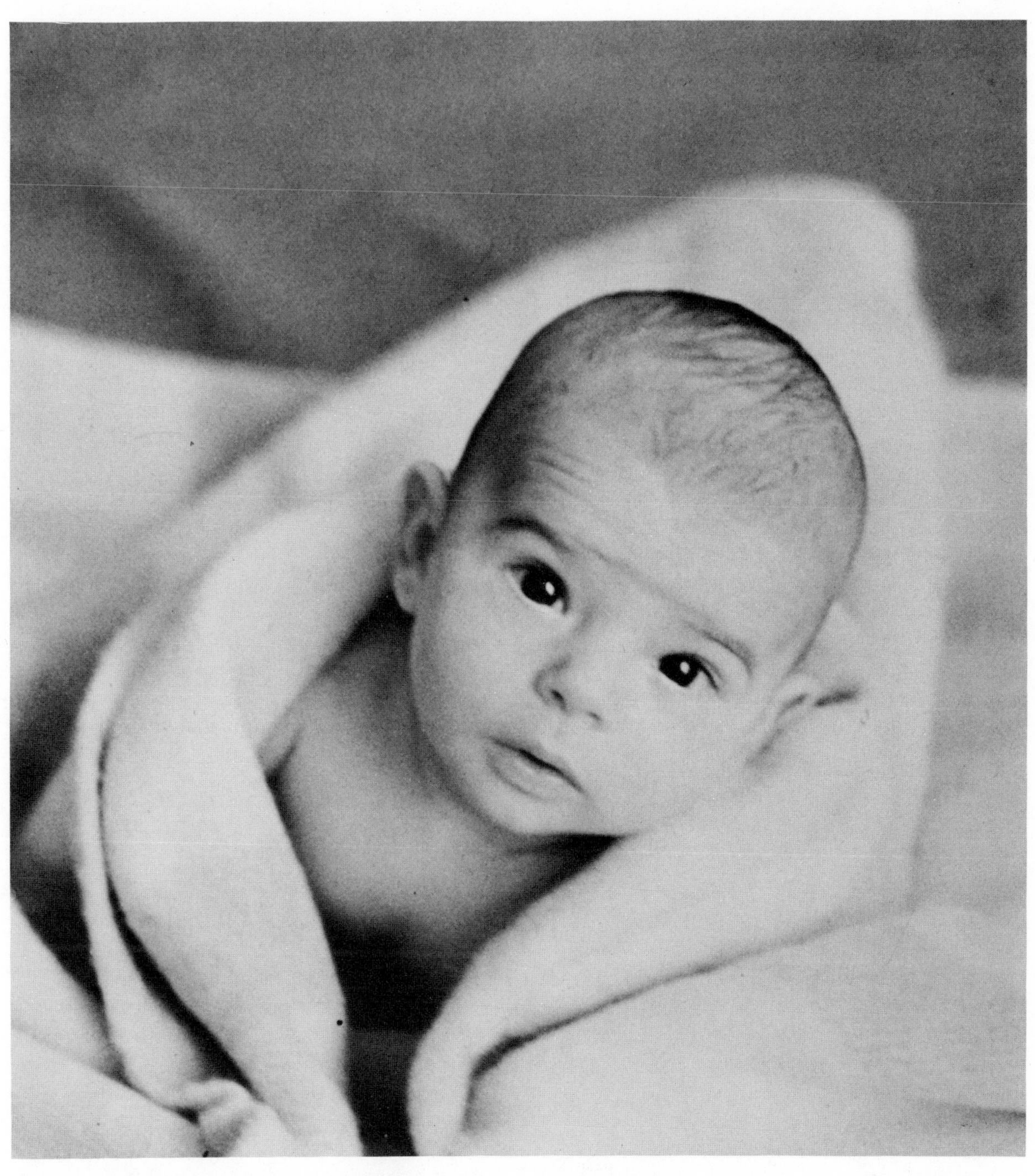

16

bring answers (except if Mommy is too busy to hear or answer them). One word even surpasses these in magic: "No," when a suggestion is made—to eat, to use the potty, to take a nap, to go to sleep. *They plead, they scold, they try to convince you.* But "No" holds out, or at least delayed actions are the result. This period, roughly from three to five years of age, is one of *negativism* as defined by the psychologist, a period that tests a mother's patience.

Although the natural curiosity may not endure through school assignments (I have yet to hear enthusiasm expressed about those), it is nevertheless not extinct. It changes direction. Children now become curious about the other sex ("Why hasn't Mary got a wee wee like mine?"), about how they were born, about how and why people die and what happens to them after death.

They also become curious about objects that stand as symbols of other objects; these cause anxiety and are not so easily talked about. PHOTOGRAPHS 17 and 18 illustrate this.

17

In the first one we see four-year-old Sophia leaning over a subway grate. Sophia is a generally well-adjusted little girl who shows an intense curiosity for all sorts of odd space configurations—dark recesses, unlighted rooms, and here, a subway grate. She hears a loud rumbling and speaks in a frightened voice of "monsters" she "sees" in her dreams. They are after her. She wants to "see them for real," but with not too much conviction; note that she is at a safe distance from the dreaded objects.

An eight-year-old playmate, PHOTOGRAPH 18, tries to convince her that there is nothing to see except the stone roof of the subway, and that the noise she hears is just the train running below it. It is obvious that he is determined to do as thorough a job of observation as can be done. Just the subway running, nothing else. But Sophia will not be convinced and tomorrow will peer again through the metal grid in hope and fear of seeing those monsters.

We have seen one-year-old Curtis curious

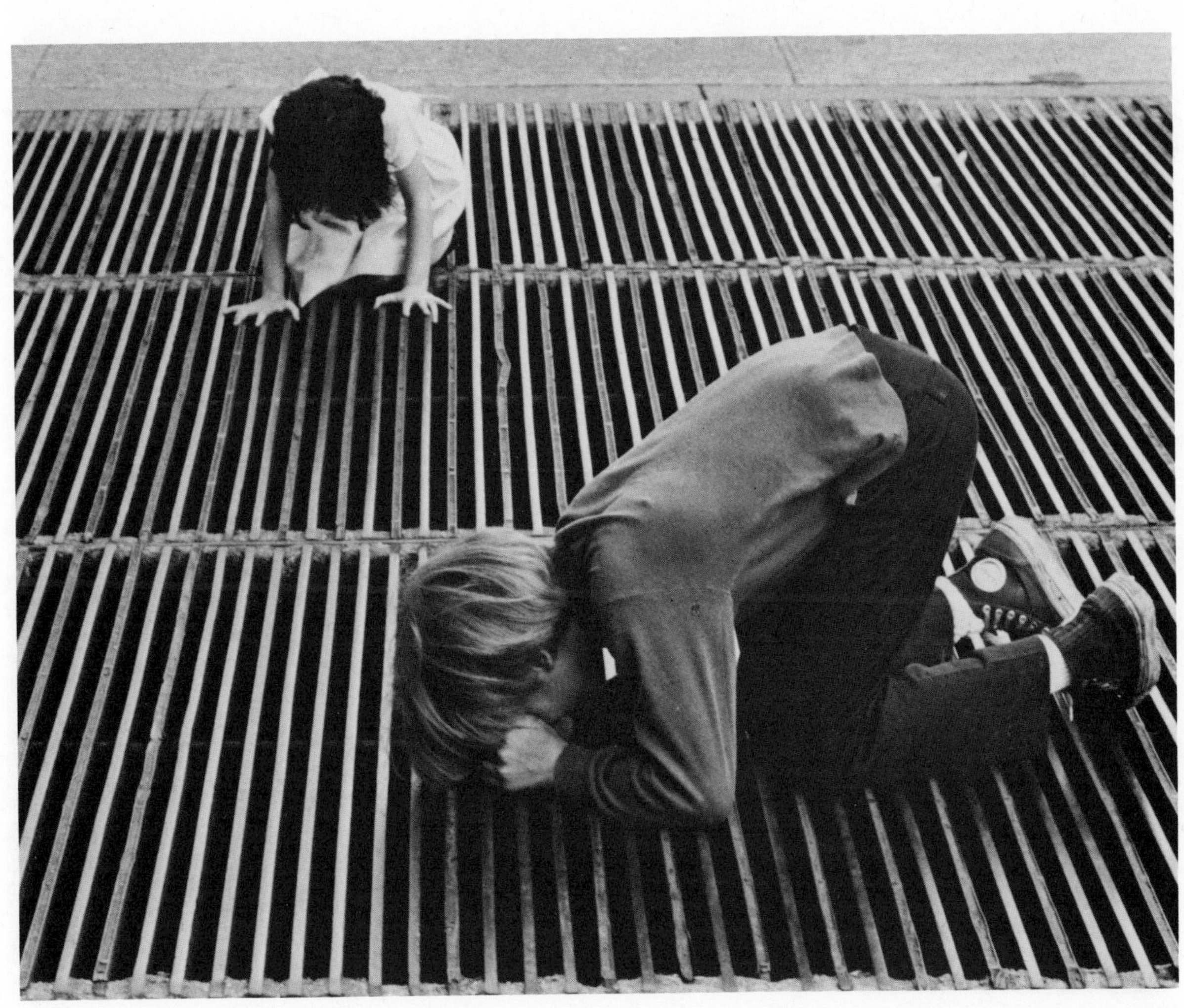

18

about a new object in his home, and what his curiosity led him to—a determined and constructive adventure. Just as determined is the two-and-a-half-year-old girl photographed at the Payne Whitney Clinic (PHOTOGRAPH 19). She has climbed onto an empty wooden case used for transferring drugs from the pharmacy to the various services. She has loosened the latch, and hopes either to remove it or to set it back where it belongs. She is precise in her movements, and were it not for her sitting on the lid, she would go further in her systematic investigation. She might even have reached this next stage, but her name was called and Mother inconsiderately picked her up to bring her to the examining pediatrician. *A grownup has no idea of the fun an old box can give you; pretty soon you would get into it and see for yourself what's hidden there.*

Now look at the four-and-a-half-year-old

19

21

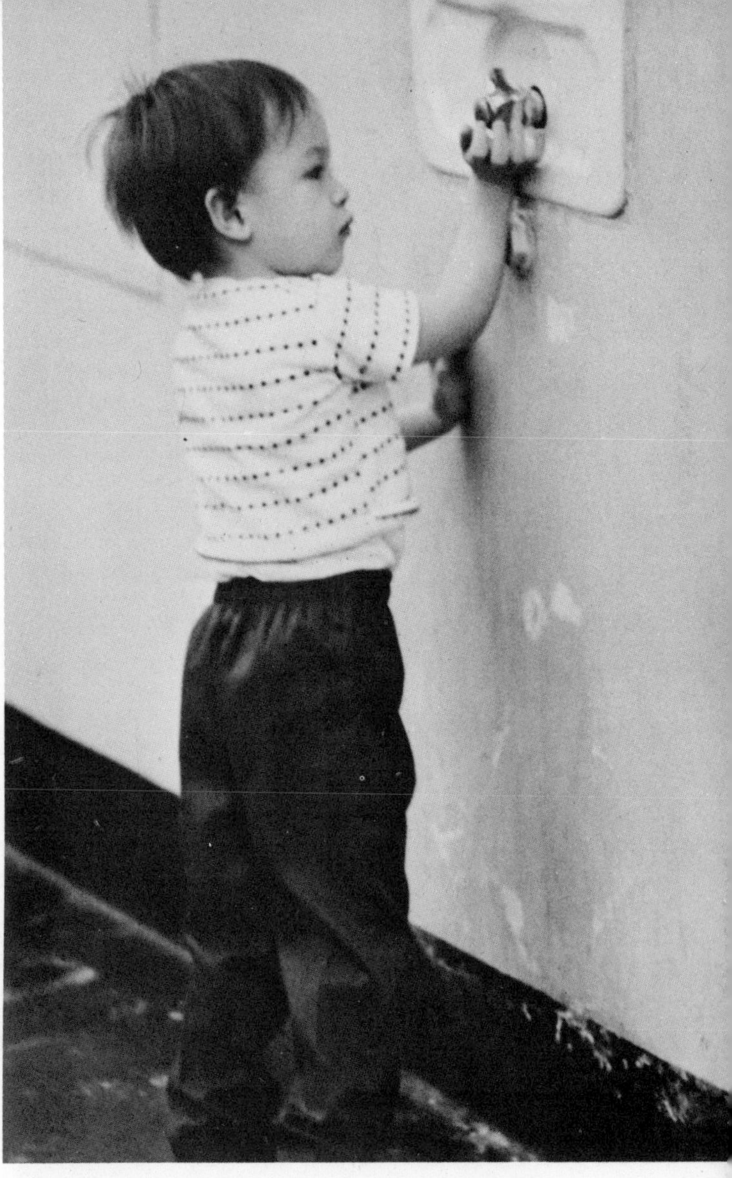

boy in PHOTOGRAPHS 20 and 21, taken at the Payne Whitney Clinic. Completely oblivious to the movement and noise about him (dozens of children and their parents are at the clinic), he concentrates with utmost seriousness on an engineering project. *How do grownups manage to get water out of this funny pipe? Right hand up, left down, that's the way they do it. But nothing comes out. It's always the same thing. If you're a grownup, you get everything, you can do everything you want. It's not fair. Ah! Maybe this square handle underneath! Maybe turn it! This way, that way.* After much experimenting, clockwise, counterclockwise, our budding engineer succeeds in producing a trickle of water that his mouth cannot reach anyway. It matters not. He has seen the water and solved a problem of capital importance to him. The smile of delight and triumph that came over his face when the fountain at long last sputtered the few drops of water reveals his satisfaction at having achieved—well, a good deal. At no point did he turn for help and the adult with him did not offer any, sensing that although he was not thirsty, he might still be curious about a water fountain.

20

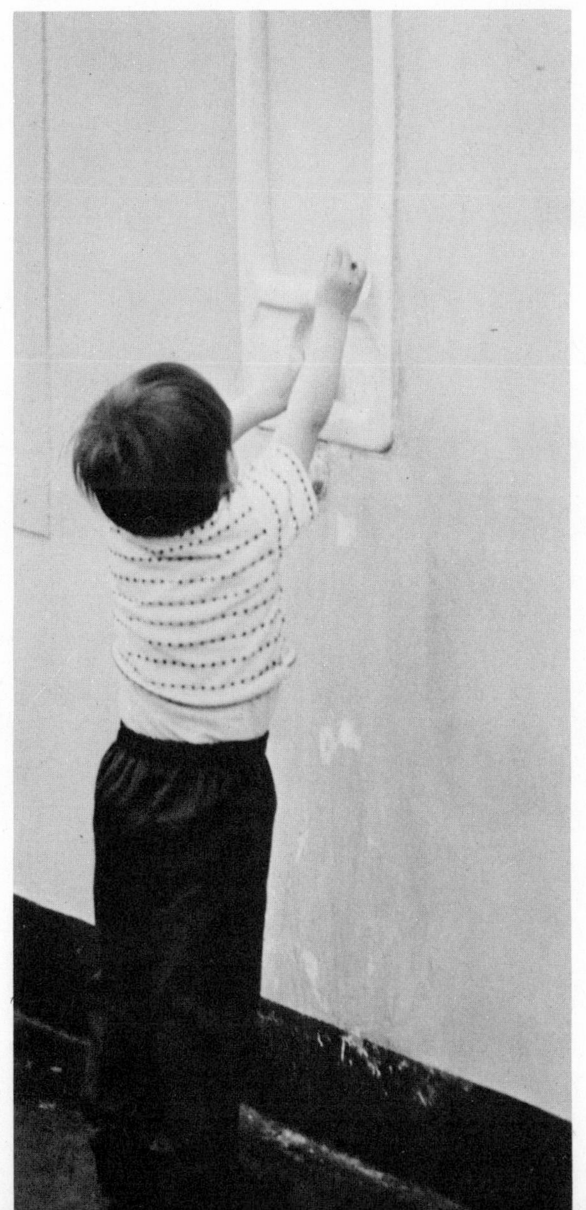

5

Leaving paradise behind

And though she be but little, she is fierce.

WILLIAM SHAKESPEARE, *A Midsummer Night's Dream*

Babyhood is a state of omnipotent living—too bad it must remain in the limbo of pre-memory. At first, only the soma remembers, then gradually the baby's experiences imprint themselves upon the growing brain. The child becomes more and more independent of the mother, beginning with improbable gait, then dashing about with or without apparent purpose.

Children get acquainted with the world around them, learn the I/not-I essential for their sense of identity. This is not done without scratches, bumps, and frustrations. They learn of the existence of others. Not they alone count now. They may have siblings whose demands often go counter to their own wishes; small playmates are introduced, and minor disciplines have to be learned. No longer is it "get and get," but rather "get and give." Learning not to have every whim anticipated and satisfied, learning to share, mean gradually to become a social being. This is not accomplished smoothly and without effort.

Rage reactions in the two- to five-year range are not uncommon; they are a normal reaction to being deprived of that "everything for me" state of bliss. However, a rage reaction which goes beyond a certain intensity leans to the abnormal. A child who cannot tolerate the least frustration—who rolls on the floor,

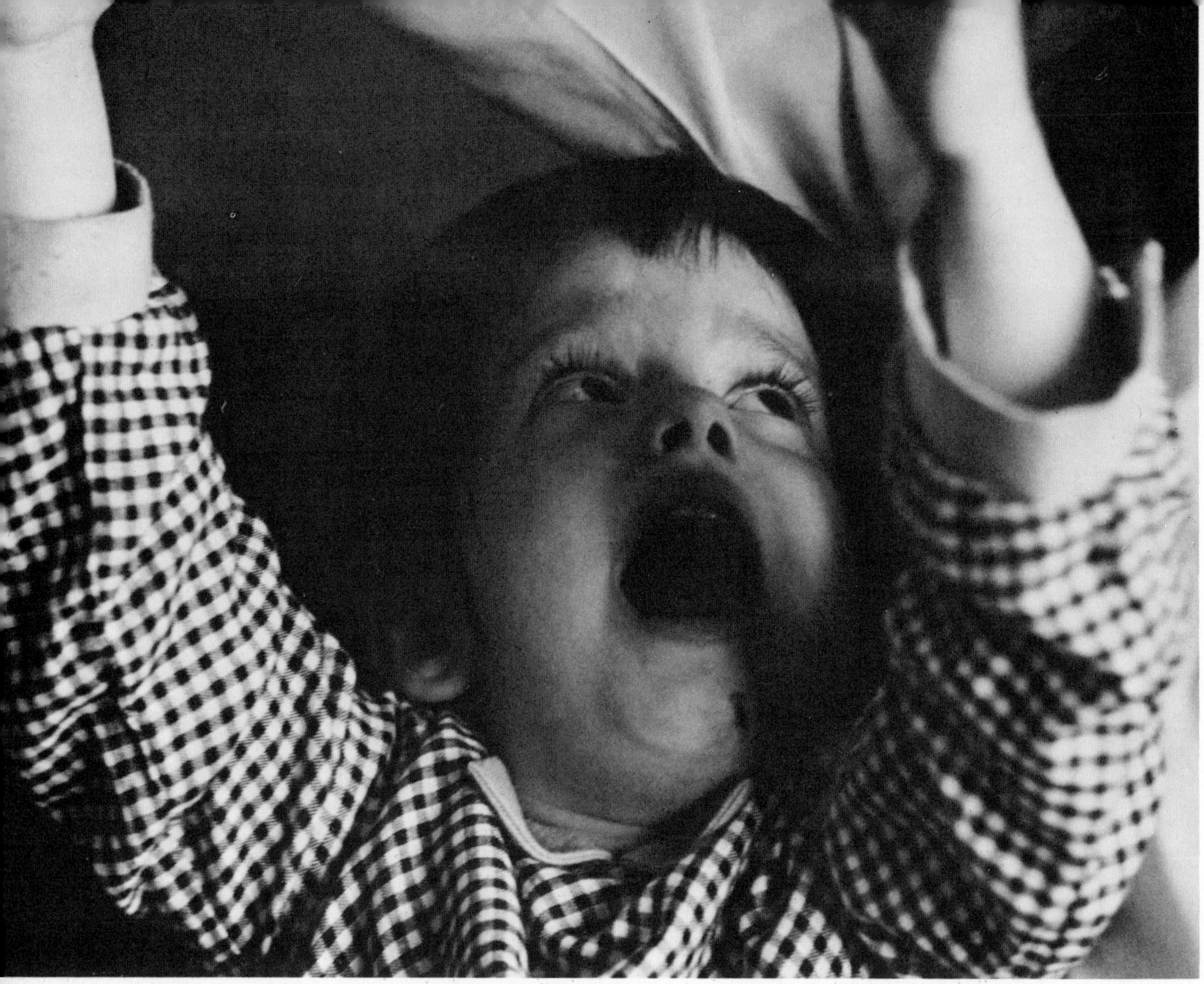

22

shrieking, unresponsive to words of affection from the mother—is overreacting.

Clara, three-and-a-half years old, has difficulty in accepting restrictions. She still entertains the belief that her every wish must be granted. In PHOTOGRAPH 22, she is seen longing to obtain her older brother's hardball. A baseball champ, he thinks of the little sister as a "pest" who prefers his belongings to her own. *How can she pitch a ball, a hardball at that, when she can't even aim at the biggest target? Besides, she throws it around the place and wrecks his games. No, she may not have his ball.* This has been made clear a number of times. But little sister will not hear, and a temper tantrum is brewing. It is not long in coming, and PHOTOGRAPHS 23 and 24 show its full explosion. The little girl's face is now so distorted by anger as to make it hardly recognizable. She is shrieking without words and it seems as though, with her hand over her mouth, she is intent on preventing words from coming out. There is grief, to be sure, but there are no tears. She can only think of the resentment accumulated against that brother of hers, but how can she tell of this now? It is the ball; she just wants the ball; she must have it this instant.

Clara has a low threshold of frustration, and frustrations are strewn in her path, or so

23

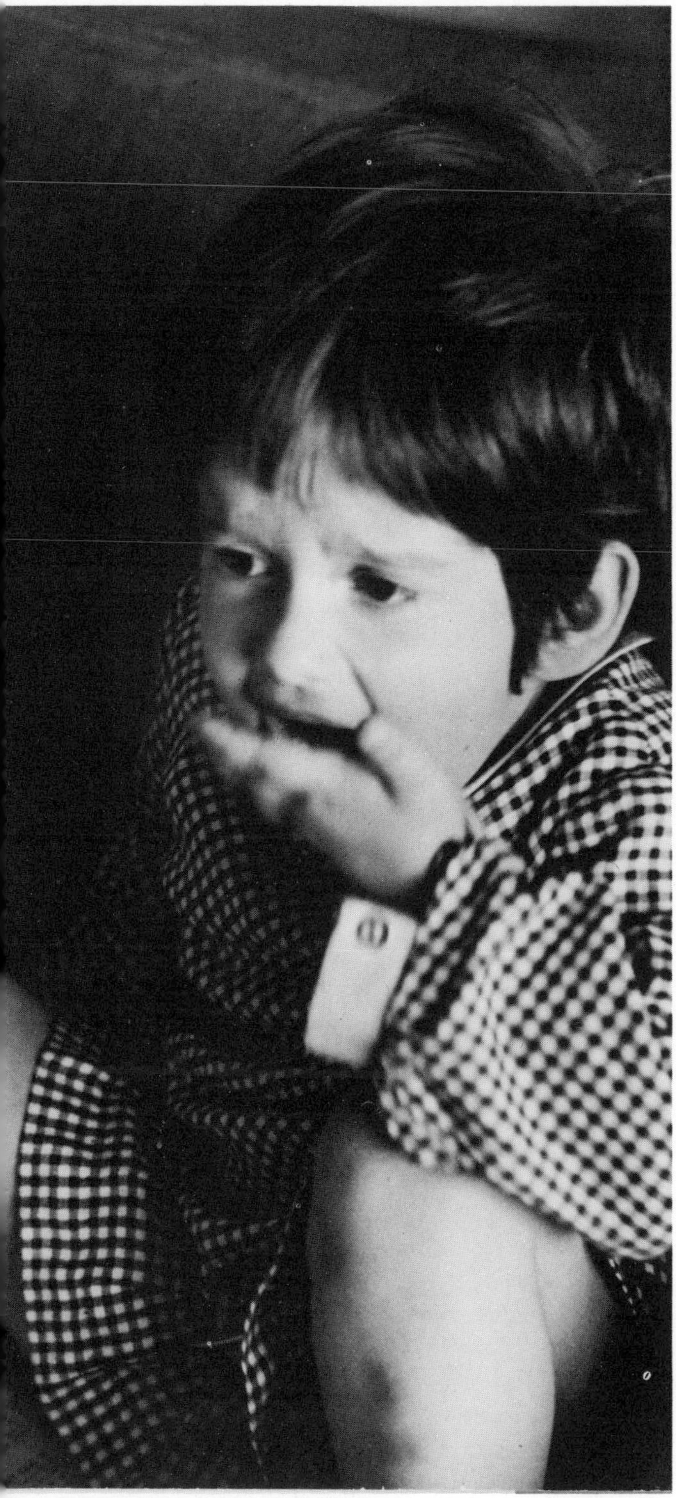

24

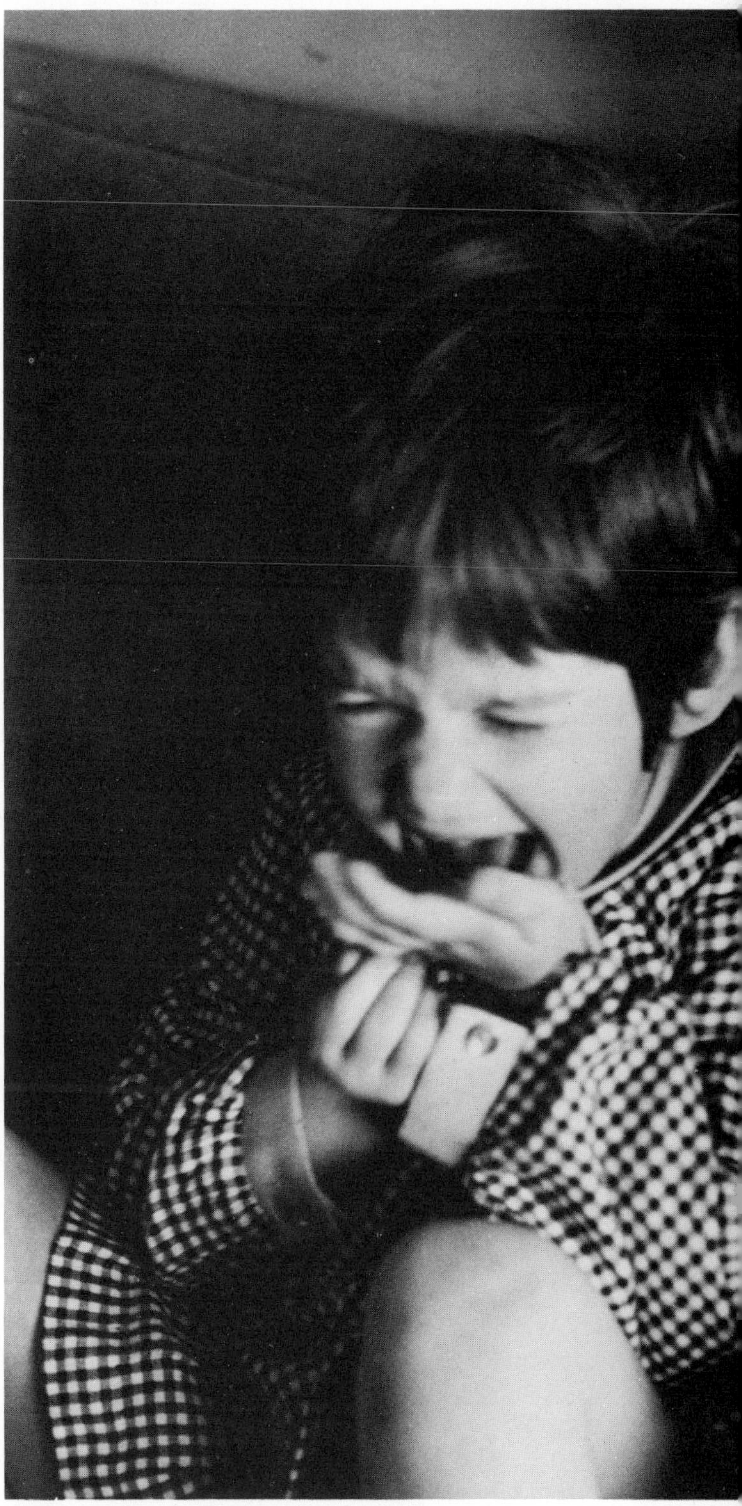

she feels. *Why do I have to have a brother, not a sister—and a big brother, not a little one—he can go to bed one hour after me—his friends come to play with him and they chase me away.* What Clara would be saying if she could interpret her disappointments is that she has not accepted Clara as Clara. The big brother seems to be getting something she does not get, just by virtue of being a boy, and older than herself to boot. Children who are insecure feel that if only they were someone else, they would be happier. They are likely to explode into rages that seem out of proportion to the immediate stimuli.

Competing with siblings, identifying with them rather than with oneself, is not an uncommon state of affairs; in various ways it leads to distortions that may become unbearable, and to a loss of interest in one's own world. I recall an eight-year-old boy who came to treatment for a severe anxiety. In the course of an early therapeutic session, while enumerating grievances he traced to his eleven-year-old brother, he suddenly stopped talking, seemed absorbed in some dark thought, then just as suddenly announced, "Do you know what I have just figured out? Even if I got to be a hundred years old, my brother would still be three years older than me. He'd be a hundred and three."

His fingers had been tapping the table during his short withdrawal, doing a double escalation of figures which had ended with the final confrontation, 100–103. This fact proved very illuminating to him, for he had lived with the myth that some day he would "catch up" with his brother. Indeed, his parents frequently told him that this would happen "with time." He was learning on his own, the hard way, that this figure of speech did not apply to time elapsed between his brother's birth and his own, as he had wished. He could still hope that it might apply to school achievement, but definitely not to years.

For Clara, accepting the big brother, a cause of so much conflict at this time, is not hopeless. Assured of her mother's love and understanding, and soon to enter nursery school, she will have the possibility of working out her resentment. Going to school will be emulating her brother; also, coming in contact with children of both sexes and slightly varying ages will bring new experiences and satisfactions.

For some children, temper tantrums can be so severe that they lose contact with reality. They "cannot be reached," and this is a serious condition requiring the attention of a skilled practitioner. Mental health and child guidance clinics are available in most communities for the recognition and treatment of such conditions.

6

Cain started it—or did he?

Thy brother came with subtilty, and hath taken away thy blessing.

Genesis, 27:35

For the first child in the family, the arrival of a second child is not an experience of unmitigated joy. For one or several years, he or she has been the sole object of the family's love and attention. Now, not only must the bounty be shared, but the child may perhaps even feel displaced by one considered an intruder. A few children are articulate about their feelings of rejection. The inner voices are then quite audible. *Take it back to the hospital—throw it in the garbage can—flush it down the toilet.* I have heard these words from children who have not accepted the new addition to the family. Does this mean that the newborn is in danger of being hurt by the older child? With a few, very few, exceptions, this is not the case. Generally speaking, the baby will be safer with a child who can voice reluctance and nonacceptance than with a sibling who looks silently at the baby with an expression of bitter hatred.

Of the several thousand children I have examined and/or treated, only one, a psychotic boy of five, had probably carried out his wish to destroy or help destroy his little brother. The baby, a few months old, was found suffocated under his blanket. The older boy, who shared a room with the baby, had been intensely jealous, staring at the infant with a smoldering look for long periods of time. In the course of his examination, he produced a wealth of drawings depicting the destruction of the baby. However, the reality and the destruction fantasies could not be disassociated in an absolute way, as would be demanded in court, for instance. A child, even a psychotic one, is not likely to say bluntly, "I killed him." Repressive forces are at work in the mentally ill as well as in the emotionally healthy child.

Children who reject a sibling may entertain destructive fantasies and may even express them freely; in fact the majority may well consider "getting rid of it." But what does a child mean when he thinks (and perhaps says), "Get rid of it"? You need only watch and listen to a group of nursery school children at play to realize that "getting rid of" is not perceived as irreversible. There is a continuous interplay of disappearing and reappearing; "I killed you" and even "I kill you dead," but also, "Now I make you 'live . . . not dead." The two phases succeed one another so rapidly that it is sometimes impossible to know whether at a given moment you're alive or dead. No matter. The next moment, you have a chance to switch to your preferred situation.

Adults have some difficulty in accepting this fluidity of the child's inner life, mostly because for them death has a finality that precludes a "comeback." We will see in Chapter 8 that to the young child death is not death at all, but a temporary void, a disappearing act to be succeeded by a reappearance. To the child, there is no faulty logic here. So, when children think or say, "Get rid of it," they do not mean "It must not live," but rather, "I don't want it." Many parents are alarmed simply because they add an adult's meaning to a child's concept. Nevertheless, sibling rivalry is an important chapter of child psychology and it cannot be dismissed as a manifestation that is negligible because it is universal. Children need support and sympathetic understanding as they face a situation that can be met only by eventual acceptance.

Parents who know of the inner voices not only accept their overt expression but encourage it by telling about their own early experiences, making it clear that it is normal and expected for the child to be upset about apparently losing something very precious. At the same time, they point out the advantages of being ahead of the little brother or sister. Sometimes, aware of the unconscious drives toward the removal of the unwanted newborn, they will enlist the child into the special care of someone as fragile as he or she once was, assigning little jobs that can be carried out with a sense of achievement and participation.

A twelve-year-old boy I treated had never forgotten a vigorous spanking he had received when he was five, reliving the painful episode with an acute intensity. Why the spanking? He had been seen "poking" at his baby brother's eyes. "I just wanted to see the color of his eyes"—a little roughly, it appears, even if the baby did not cry. The aggressive impulse behind the curiosity could be easily perceived, but let it be noted that his being kept away from the baby "for fear he would harm him" had only increased his desire to do the thing so laboriously forbidden—get close enough to the baby to touch him, to push and pull him. These aggressive impulses toward the sibling are not without a sense of guilt which registers as a sad, sometimes depressed facial expression.

Of interest is an observation relating to the birth of a third child. The first-born is likely to welcome the third with open joy; he or she is no longer threatened, and the guilt toward the second child finds some relief in the acceptance of the youngest. This is a well-known pattern, one which can be anticipated and which is reassuring to parents, who generally believe that the arrival of the third child will aggravate matters for the oldest.

The drama briefly outlined here is clearly illustrated in these photographs. The fourth birthday of Sally, the little girl in a striped dress, is being celebrated with a children's party. The mother, busy with the management of the party, has placed on a bench the crib in which her latest-born is sleeping. In PHOTOGRAPH 25, Sally immediately turns to him with interest and delight while her two-year-old brother, Jamie, is not only reluctant to join her, but is so unhappy that five-year-

25

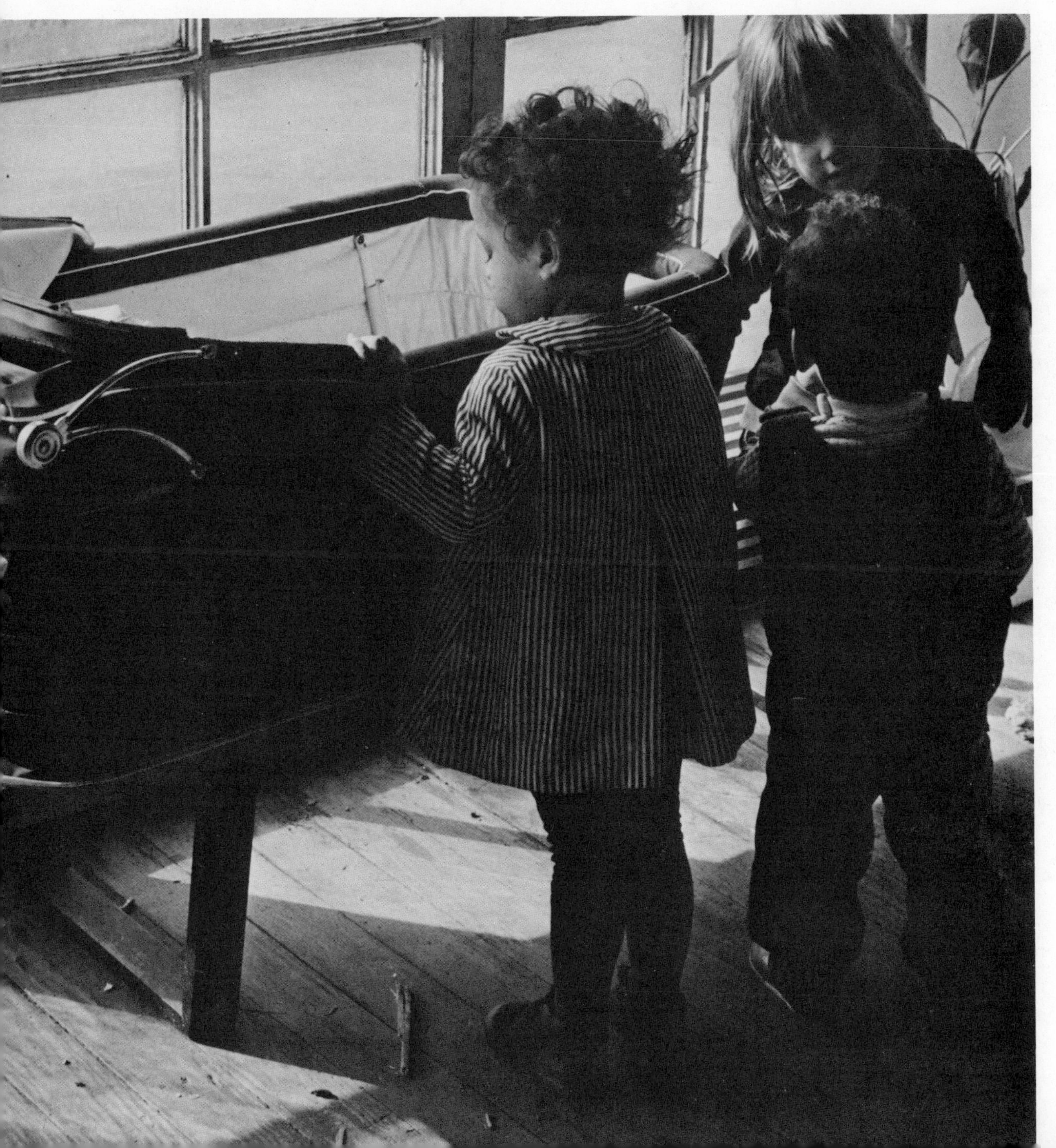

old Jenny tries to entertain him as best she can. In PHOTOGRAPH 26, when Jenny has given up her comforter's job, he stands near the crib, dejected. Although he is generally not a finger sucker, you can see him busy seeking comfort with a good deal of his right hand in his mouth. *What is so great about that baby? And why is Sally so crazy about him? She was not so nice with me—two was enough—send him back—get him out and maybe Sally will smile at me like she does at him.* In PHOTOGRAPH 27, Jamie has given up, abandoned by sister and friend as well. Nothing left but to sulk and suck. But see the radiant look on Sally, who finds it exhilarating to have another little brother. No danger for her of a repeat performance of the jealousy that is now tormenting Jamie.

26

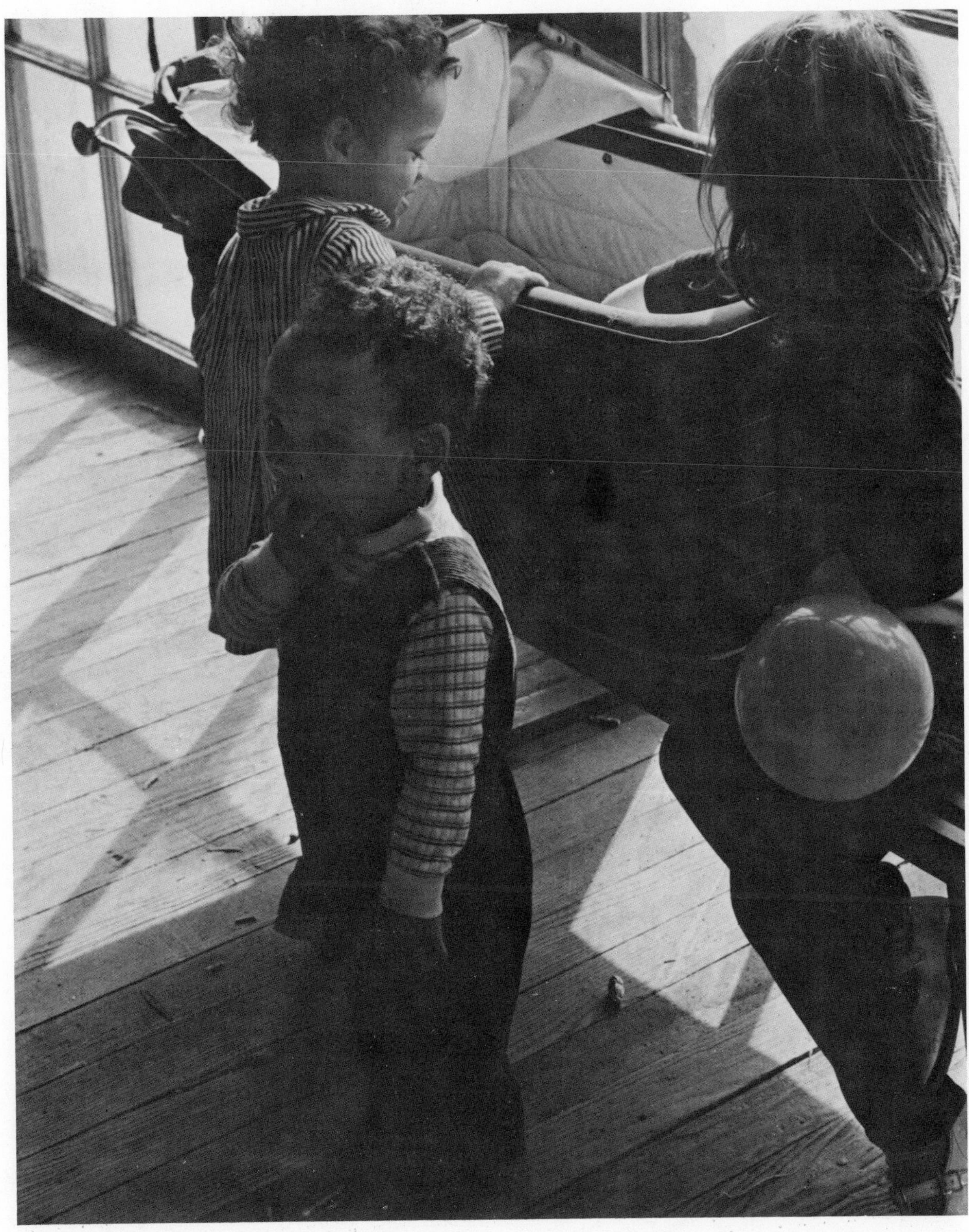

27

7

Not so easy, this business of "when" and "where"

> After all, it doesn't amuse me very much to make mud-pies, to scribble, to perform my natural functions: in order for these to have value in my eyes, at least one grown-up must go into raptures over my products.
>
> JEAN-PAUL SARTRE, *The Words*

Being a child psychiatrist presents certain advantages in acquiring an understanding of the emotionally *healthy* child. Often, though not always, the history of a troubled child points unmistakably to a blind spot in his or her training which is responsible for difficulties encountered in later years. Bowel training is among the sensitive areas because it can be a source of conflict between two personalities, the mother and the child, with a strong emotional interaction between them. In addition, physical readiness on the part of the child is necessary.

Although physical readiness cannot be set at an absolute age level, it can be approximated as occurring within the range of eight to fifteen months, allowing for individual differences in the rate of motor development. The back muscles must be strong enough to permit the sitting position. Some babies reach this stage at six months, while others, also normal in their growth, are not ready until a year, or older. These are extremes, but can be considered starting points for any rational attempts at "training." Some mothers are proud of having achieved results aimed at as early as eight months; a few have stated bluntly that they "started at birth."

In general, precociousness is a boost to parental pride, but must it be demonstrated

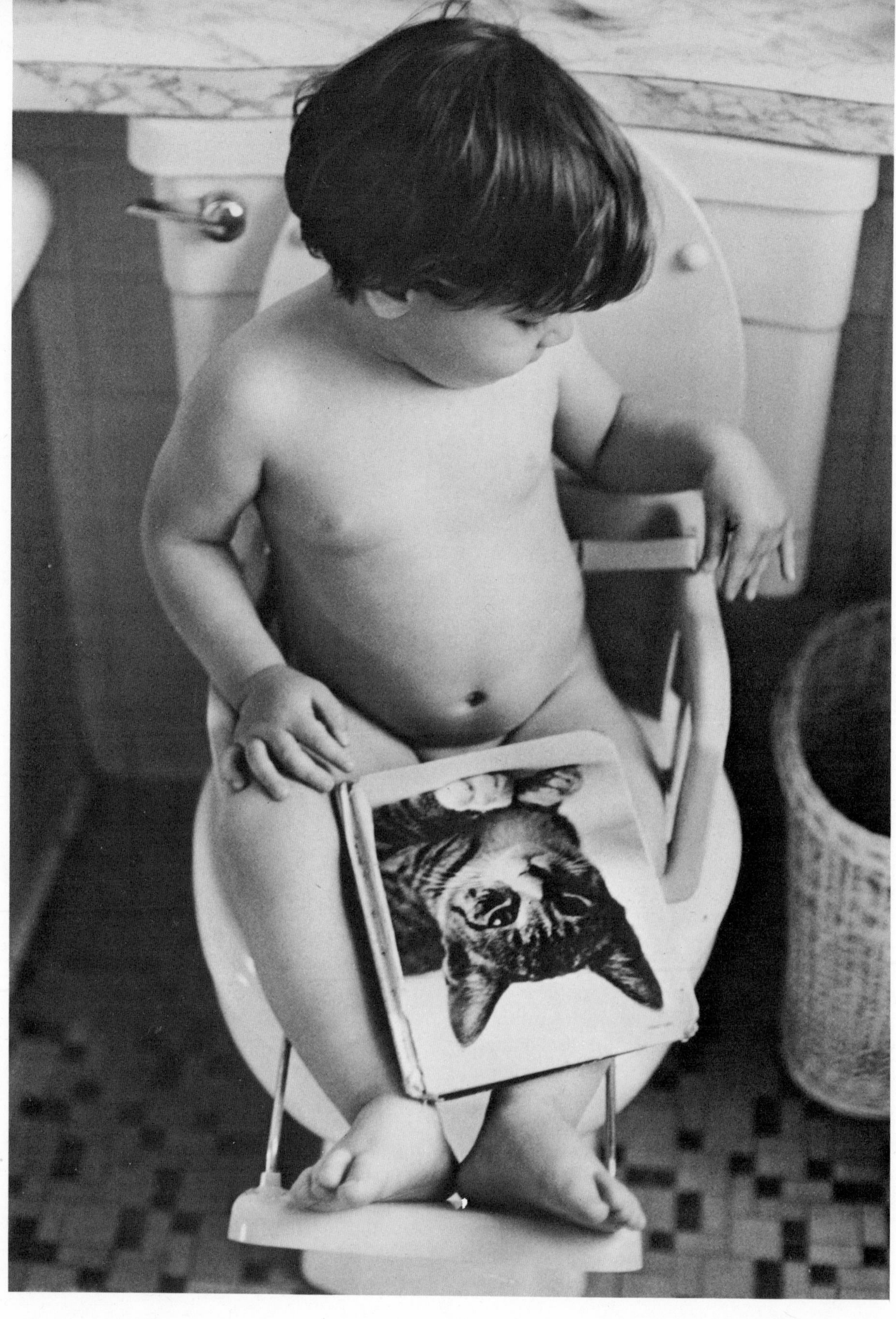

28

29

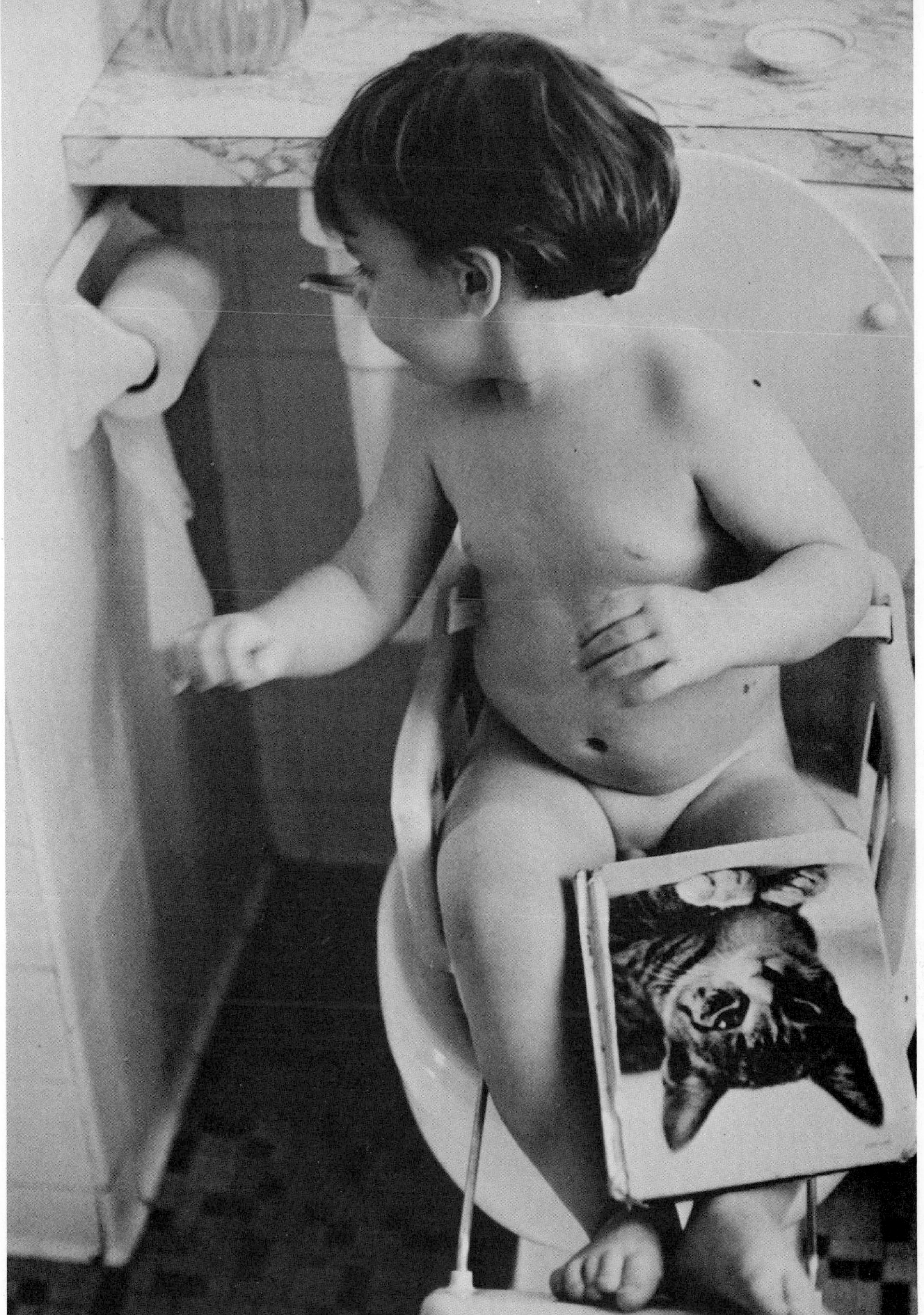

30

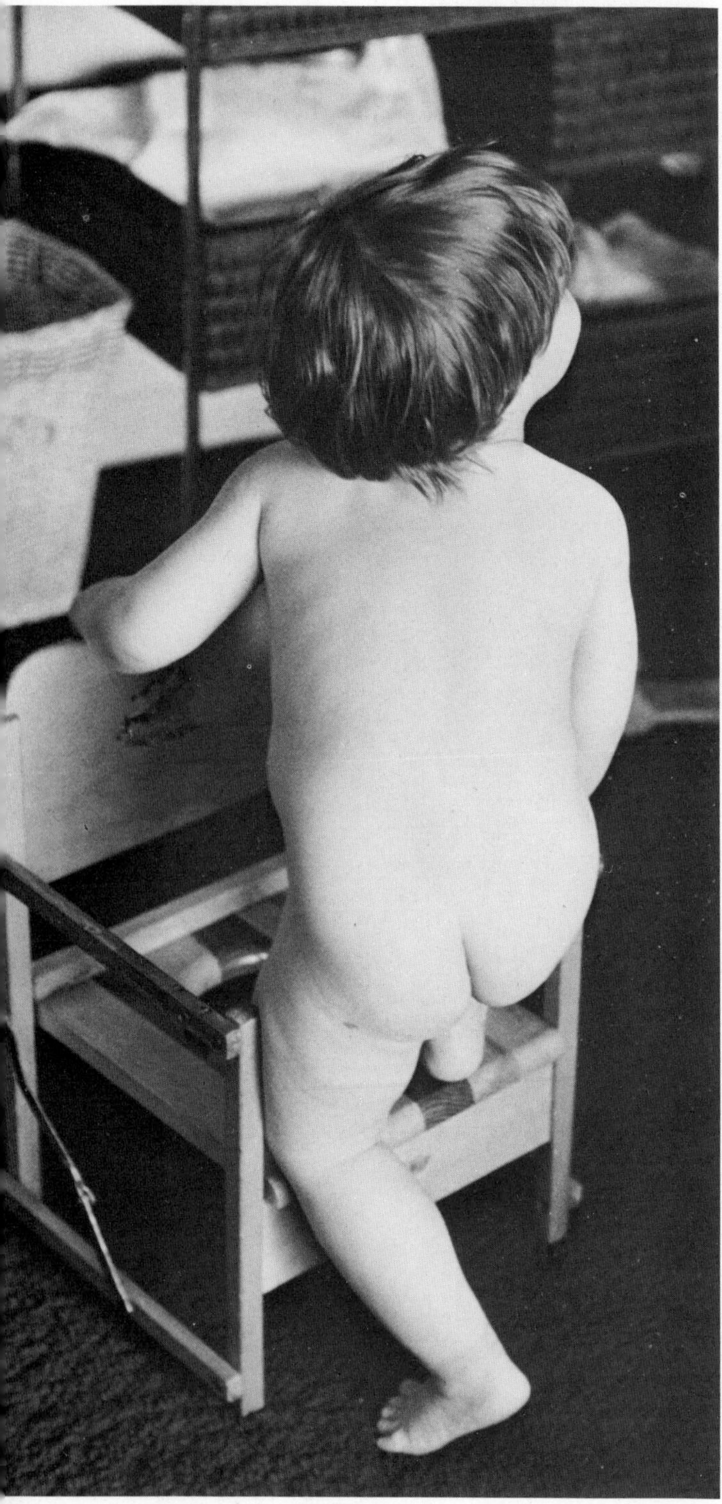

in the area of bowel discipline? The cost is too great in terms of the rigidity and compulsiveness of the resulting behavior, the resistance to other disciplines. Fortunately, excessive zeal on the part of the modern mother is much less in evidence than was formerly the case—in Victorian times, for instance. We know, through the psychoanalytic methods of investigation and therapy, that young children are reluctant to let go of what they consider part of themselves, and that over-insistent adults only increase their resistance to training. Rigid demands are repaid with self-defeat, as well as with neurotic behavior on the part of the child.

Adam is an eighteen-month-old boy, a magnificent physical specimen (his back muscles are certainly strong enough) who is still resisting training. His noncompliance has been good-humored, with a touch of facetiousness. In PHOTOGRAPH 28, we see that he has been enticed to try the adult toilet fitted with a baby seat. His favorite cat picture has come along. But what is Adam interested in? A small spot near the belt has caught his attention, a spot just discovered and now all-absorbing. Even the cat is neglected. *What is all this fuss about doody? Why should it be in that big hole? You can go down the toilet, even if Mommy says "No, it can't happen." The potty is safer. No flushing.* (Adam, strong and sure of himself as he may appear, has expressed the fear that he, not only the stool, could be washed down.) He sits, looks around for a diversion—and there it is: the roll of toilet paper, exclusive possession of the adults. In PHOTOGRAPH 29, he starts on a bout of yanking at the roll which will be of no use to him anyway. Oblivious of his mother's urging and chatty small talk, he continues his exploration. No, there is nothing further to expect here.

The potty chair has not proved more of a

31

success as a proper seat for the demanded performance (PHOTOGRAPHS 30 and 31). Adam views it as a prized piece of equipment, a miniature gymnasium built for his enjoyment. Mini-acrobatics are in order. And that is about all you can get from Adam at this point. No, he won't try here and now. Any place, any time, when he feels like it, but not on request, even from that patient and smiling mother of his.

The parents have heard the message, but they don't worry. They know that he is a happy, well fed, cheerful youngster; they let him go at his own pace, in the hope that some day, possibly very soon, he will respond to his mother's rather timid suggestions. Subsequent information is that he has done exactly that without coercion, bribery, or threats, and he does not even exhibit any pride. Entirely matter of fact—in his eyes it is not even an achievement.

8

Maybe everybody, but not me

And weeping fast as she had breath
Janet implored us, "Wake her from her sleep!"
And would not be instructed in how deep
Was the forgetful kingdom of death.

JOHN CROWE RANSOM, *Janet Waking*

A simple child,
That lightly draws its breath,
And feels its life in every limb,
What should it know of death?

WILLIAM WORDSWORTH, *We Are Seven*

Incredible as they may seem, the words of this chapter title are spoken or thought by most young children when they first grasp the reality of death. Long before that, they may have used the words "kill" and "die" profusely, in games, fantasies, and stories exchanged with their peers. At that early stage, no one believes in it. There is something magical about the on and off of the killing game, and even if a close relative dies, the child does not associate the disappearance with the killing-game fantasies.

As a rule, young children become acquainted with death when a pet animal dies, whether it be their own or a friend's. They experience great grief when a pet dog is run over, or even when a hamster dies in a more natural way. The projection is always, "What about me?" If an older relative, a grandfather for instance, dies, even if they have had little to do with him, they project themselves vividly enough to feel that if it happens to grandfather, it can happen to them. Yet, they may still fail to "visualize" what dying means. They even rebel against the idea that, though he is very old, the grandfather is dying.

One nine-year-old girl, whose grandmother died after a short illness, became infuriated at God for having taken her grandmother away. True, this was a period when the

32

theme, "God is dead," was flaunted as a novel concept, and children watching television programs were deeply stirred by it. She raged, cried, stamped her feet, refusing to accept her grandmother's death and accusing God.

It is usually possible to alleviate on a realistic basis some of the fears that children have about their own death (it always comes down to that) by indicating that as people

33

live longer and grow older, as their interests and their strength lessen, it is hard for them to go on, and they do not fight the idea of death as a child naturally does.

Gregory, a seven-year-old New York City boy, has so far had no acquaintance with the phenomenon of death. He frequently goes to the country on weekends, and in PHOTOGRAPH 32 he is starting out on a familiar jaunt to join his friends. At this moment he has no other preoccupation than to get to his friend's house. His step is rhythmic, lively, as if he were on a march. With lush vegetation, trees, and grass all around him, he is unconcerned with his surroundings, intent only on his goal. Suddenly he stops (PHOTOGRAPH 33). On the ground, lifeless, is a bird he knows to be a blue jay, one of his favorites. He is very troubled by the sight and ponders over it. He must find out what has happened. He leans over (PHOTOGRAPH 34) and picks up the dead bird although he is a little squeamish about it.

34

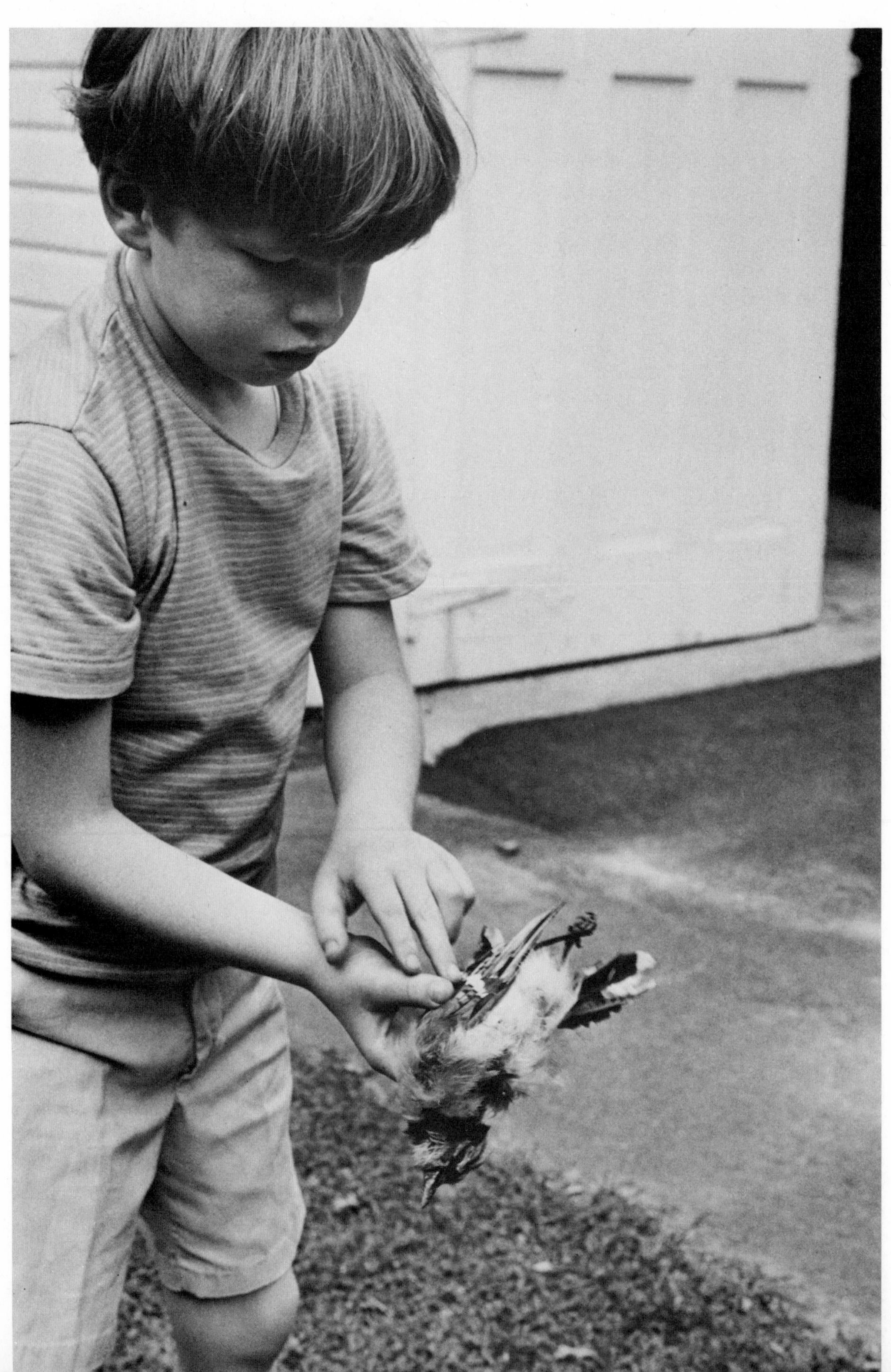

35

In PHOTOGRAPH 35, he seems to seek comfort from the colors, still bright. *Look at those beautiful feathers, they are live; the bird is going to fly again; maybe.* The discovery shakes him, but finally he must recognize that the end has come for his friend, the blue jay. It was with great reluctance that he had picked up the bird, and his expression throughout shows that he is in the presence of an alien phenomenon. It is hard for him to accept that this limp, mangled bird, once so beautiful, can never come back and fly. But disturbed though he is, he has still not gotten the full impact of the death reality.

Gregory is a little older than most children when hit by this reality, but his reaction is fairly typical. It is primarily one of non-acceptance. The situation becomes most difficult to handle when a friend or classmate dies. A five-year-old boy, bright, gay, very popular in his nursery group, was suddenly taken ill and died of septicemia in two days. It was impossible to hide the fact from the children because they had seen the troubled look on the faces of the child's mother, the teachers, and even their own mothers. At a time when they cannot themselves foresee that they will also die, children rebel totally against the idea that a person could die very young. It had to be explained that young people can also, but *very, very rarely,* die when they have become *very, very sick* and the doctors do not know how to treat the illness because the drug for it has not yet been found. A pall of depression was noticeable among the children for several days and from time to time they persisted in asking when Johnny would come back.

I remember the reaction of a young boy, then six years old, who fiercely rejected the suggestion that he, too, would die, in a faraway future, of course. An uncle had recently died, and for the first time he conjured up the possibility of his own eventual end. "No," he said, "I won't die. Methuselah lived until he was a thousand years old. That guy in Turkey lived to four hundred, and in the paper there was something about a guy in Russia who died at a hundred-fifty." These vital statistics may not be conspicuous for their accuracy, but the faith is there. Anybody else, but not himself. To an adult, such reasoning is irrational. Children have reasoning of their own.

9

The grownups say "It's a great life," and that's what it is for real

Le bonheur de l'enfant est celui de la rose
Qui fait ses perles d'un peu d'eau.
RENÉ SULLY PRUDHOMME, *A la Nuit*

Have you ever had the chance to walk behind a toddler along a street, say in New York City? A stream of people are coming from the opposite direction and you notice that they all smile as they look down. The paunchy, past-middle-age executive, the window washer, the young housekeeper, the office worker, anyone who comes along will react thus to our little toddler. What is the reason for this universal response? What is the secret behind the ability of this young life to bring a look of joy—however fleeting—into the faces of all who see it? Five- or six-year-olds might arouse interest with their antics or their arresting behavior, but the reaction is not guaranteed to be one of amused interest on the part of all passersby. What characterizes the younger child is a Promise—the Promise of a life that is yet to unfold, with overtones of dynamics, adventure, gusto, and, hopefully, a minimum of frustration. In the background there is the question, "Will the Promise be fulfilled?"

Young children are so accustomed to this reaction, on the part of strangers as well as familiars, that they are actually disturbed by its absence or the negative reaction of an outsider who may for personal reasons show divergence from the general pattern. I have in mind a four-year-old girl who, finding herself in an elevator with a patient who was obviously depressed, stood agog and mute, waiting until she got out of the elevator to ask, "What is the matter with that lady? She looks funny." She was not able to make a diagnosis, but unknowingly she had made one. If people do not react with the usual smile, it must be that they are "funny"—a word that children use, with generosity, to mean "different," unlike any other.

Young children evidence joy at just being alive, which means *you can wrap yourself around your mother's neck, tiny fingers digging into her skin; you put your foot forward and your whole body moves; you stretch your arm and reach out for some object you want; you gulp the milk or mush that your mother has prepared;* and the thousand other small activities which make up the life of young children. All of this is evidenced in the expression that radiates from their faces and makes people, otherwise indifferent, respond with a smile.

In PHOTOGRAPH 36 we have our little Victoria, who at two months has not only mastered a technique but benefited from her mother's own learning in the same area. She is now a veteran suckler and enjoying life as she never did before. Look back at the earliest photographs of Victoria in Chapter 2. She was not then what you would call a happy baby. Now her interests have widened. Everything around her stimulates her. She has a zest for life which was in no way evident in the past. All the paraphernalia used for the physical care of a baby are in front of her. She might be interested in some items were it not that the man with the camera is also in front of her, and she is intrigued by his activities. With an unfamiliar person moving

36

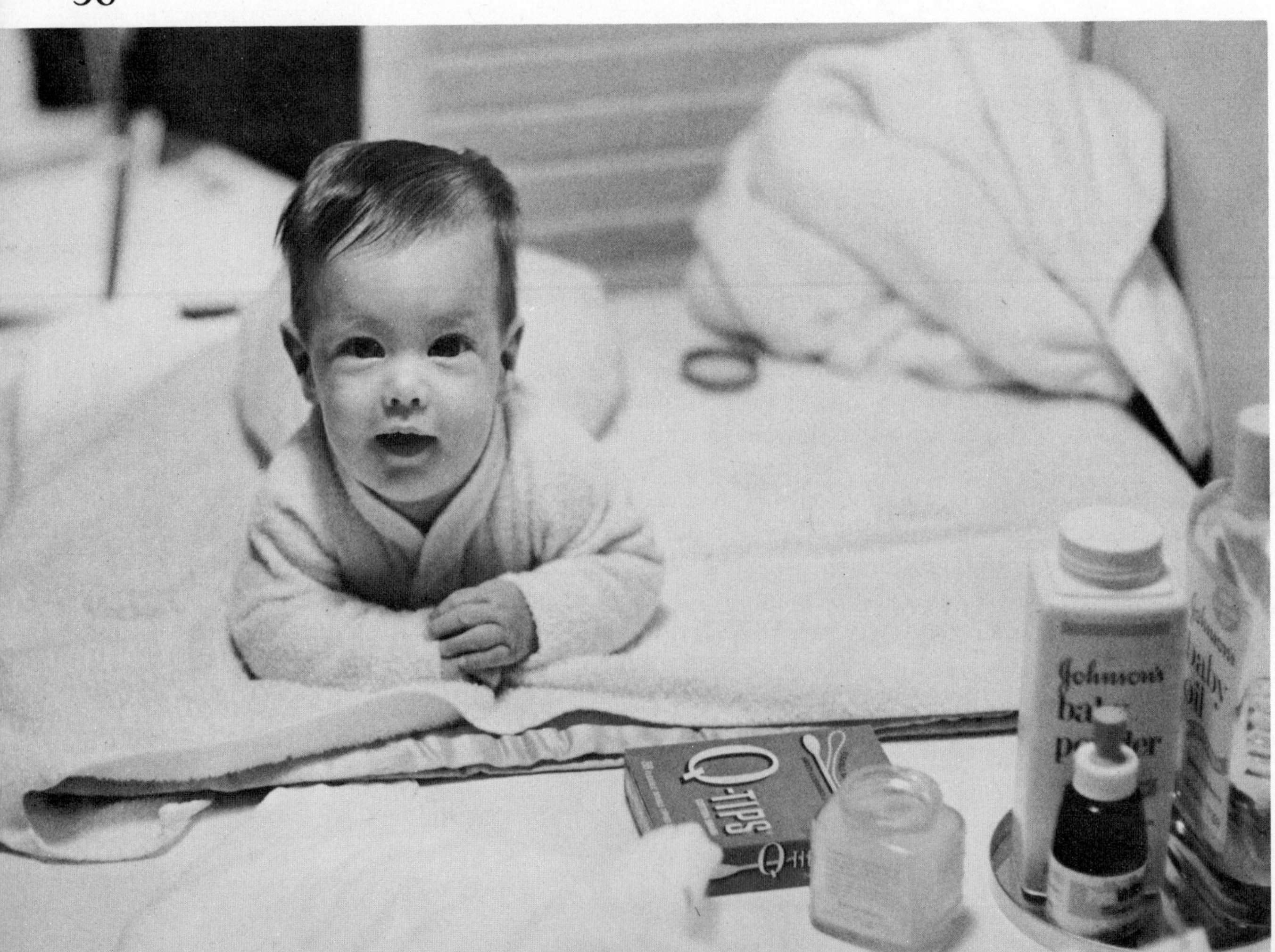

37

about, Q-tips, vaseline, and baby powder are for the moment completely ignored. It is quite evident that Victoria is a changed baby.

In PHOTOGRAPHS 37 and 38 we again find little one-year-old Curtis, who was so intent on his conquest of forbidding heights in Chapter 3. It might be difficult to find a child more bursting with the desire to see, to grasp, to get in touch with, to move one's limbs, to conquer space by any and all means, and at the same time reaching out for the love and affection of people around him. Remember what his nurse said about him—"He is all mouth and hands." Succinct as this is, it is a very good description of Curtis's relation to his world. This is a happy, well-adjusted youngster.

There is no difficulty in interpreting Curtis's inner thoughts since they are clearly projected in every picture. Note that he is not trying to entertain his audience. He finds his own fun in every situation. It is good to have interested spectators, but at the present time he does not have an imperative need of them. A deliberate choice of crawling when he is quite able to walk demonstrates his independence; he is determined to go it his own way. There are unlimited possibilities within reach. The effort and the reaching bring on the luminous, broad smile with which we have become familiar. In PHOTOGRAPH 37 Curtis seems to be ready for a leapfrog jump. With his smiling attitude toward life, he can only bring smiles in return—and what fun it is to crawl (if one can call throwing oneself through the air "crawling"). Indeed, PHOTOGRAPH 38 shows a foot that reaches a commendable height too fast for the camera to focus on it. Children, even very young ones, have wanted to fly solo since long before planes were invented; they consistently dream about it.

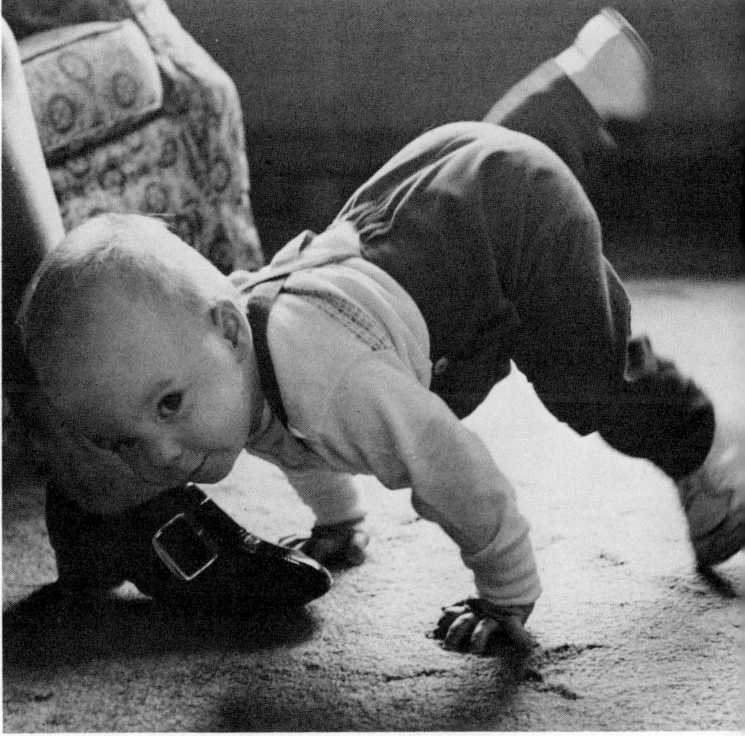

38

In PHOTOGRAPH 39, we see the same explosion of joy at just being free to roam in and get acquainted with the outside world. Feet bare, scantily clothed on a sunny day, four-year-old Tracy starts on a flight which promises to be all joy. This exuberance is characteristic of young children who are healthy, well fed, and loved.

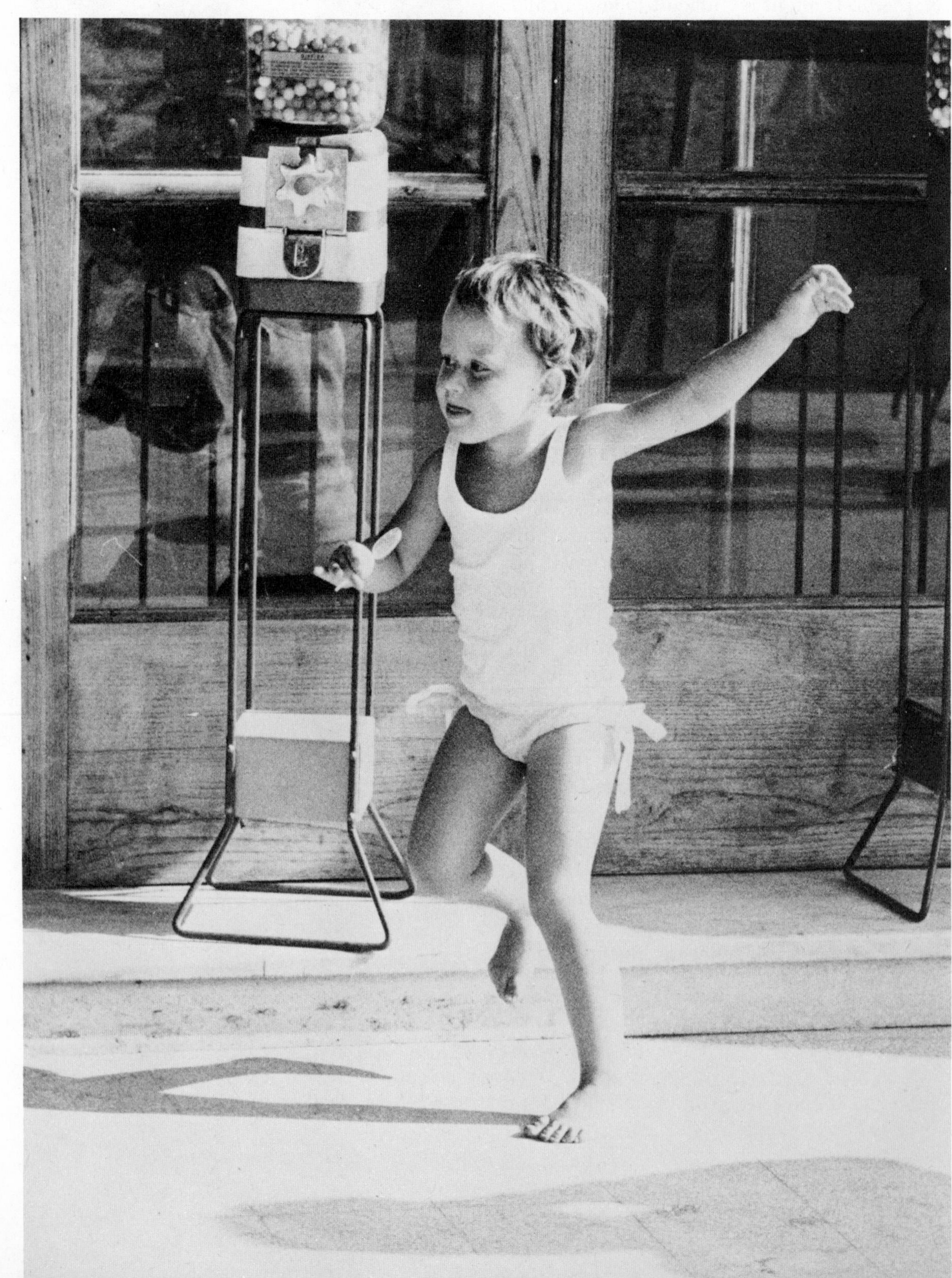

39

40

In the next photographs, we see children keenly involved in some favorite activities. In PHOTOGRAPHS 40 and 41, two brothers are on an exploration trip with their friends. Although they are not very far from the ground, they see themselves as mountain climbers. The five-year-old is so satisfied with his escalation that he pauses to contemplate the abyss below his feet. Everything stimulates their interest: the leaves of low trees, the grass, the stones, big tree trunks to be hurdled.

41

42

In PHOTOGRAPH 42, a large construction project seems to be in the offing; no need of an architect or supervisor to direct operations. The wonderful wet sand can be built into forts, castles, walls—and what's more, it can be smeared all over one's body.

Sand can be used for other fantasies, as we can see in PHOTOGRAPH 43. The five-year-old boy sitting in a rowboat at rest on the edge of the water is seen operating the oar with great satisfaction. It does not matter that only the sand moves, and ever so little. He has the complete illusion that he could go very far out with this embarkation. The adult responsible for the boy has thought it safe to leave him on land as he certainly would not have the muscular power to free the boat. No matter. The young explorer is launching a real trip on the ocean. To adult eyes, this boat may not be moving; but to the young sailor, it has gone many knots (though he doesn't know this word).

43

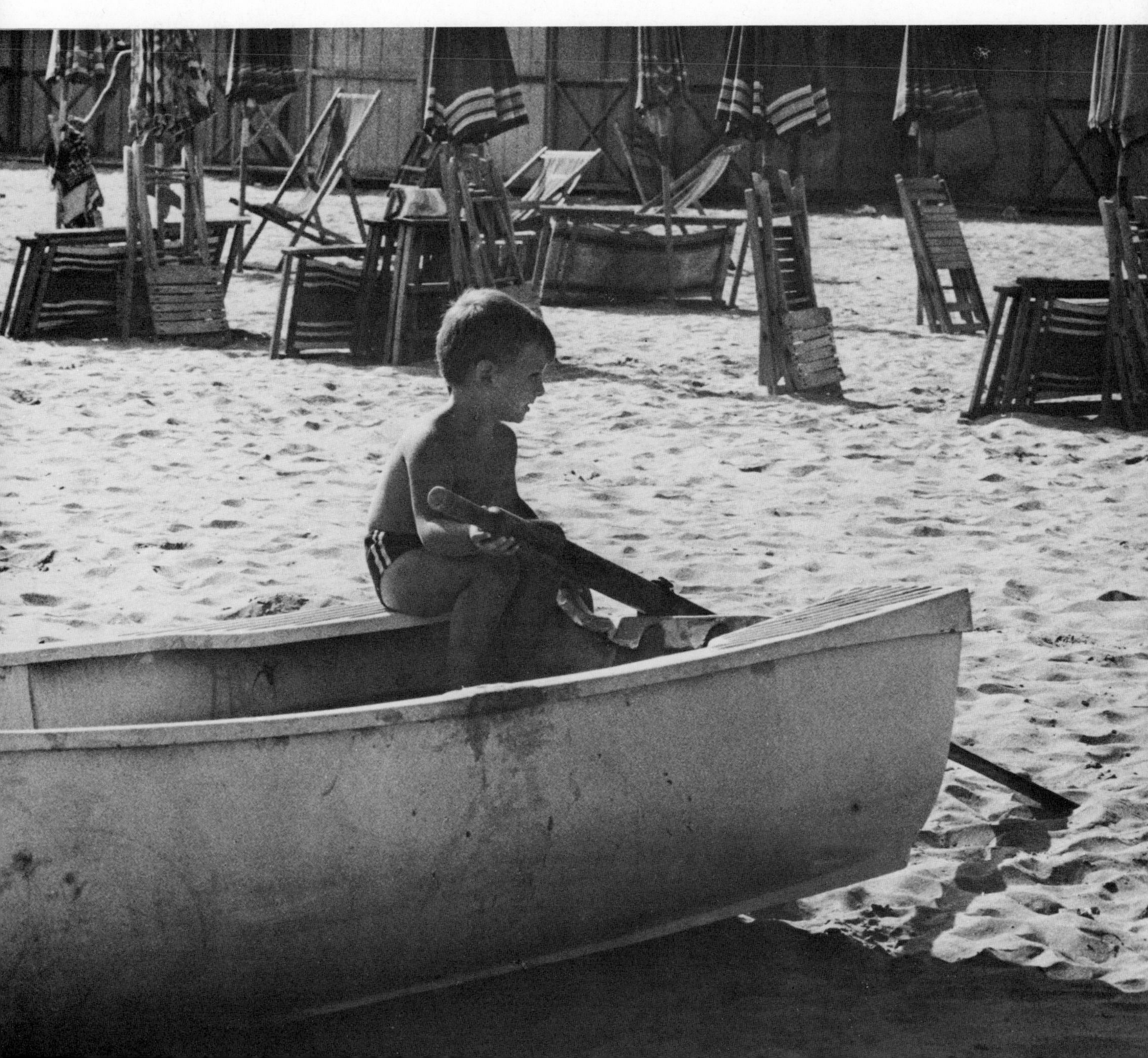

In PHOTOGRAPH 44, taken in Italy, seven children, boys and girls, are starting out on a cycle trip with their eyes undoubtedly on the Tour, a favorite European athletic competition. Boys in Europe, long before their teens, fantasy success on the Tour just as an American boy who shadowboxes sees himself as a second Muhammad Ali. The cyclists have chosen as a leader a slightly older girl with a somewhat larger and better equipped bicycle—or perhaps she just started in the lead. She certainly stands there as Queen of the Road (one step ahead of the Tour, which admits only men for the tough competition). The bicycles are not too rapid, but each child probably fantasies being a Tour winner.

Many of the photographs have projected children in their relation to space. All young children fantasy themselves as flyers. We have mentioned a boy who, impersonating Superman, had taken a flight from his father's high dresser with disappointing results. The reality seldom matches the fantasy. The location need not be so specific. Almost anywhere, children can pretend that they are in flight. See, for instance, PHOTOGRAPH 45. A six-year-old boy has been on the ice for some time and feels quite secure on his skates. At the moment, he appears to be flying through space, which gives him great satisfaction; indeed he has become a fiend for space. His happy expression is evidence of his victory. His pants, torn at the knees, bear witness to earlier attempts, but he is now really a flyer. The moon may not be his next step, but a plane!—just give him time.

44

45

It is in general true that unloved, unwell, or ill-fed children do not show the exuberance and zest for life seen in the comfortably situated children whose photographs have appeared in this chapter. Anyone familiar with the plight of underprivileged children will have observed the apathy that replaces ebullience. Yet deprived children often find their own way to enjoy living, to create their own amusements—this with a tenacity and ingenuity one can only marvel at. In PHOTOGRAPH 46, taken in Bangkok, a two-and-a-half-year-old boy is seen in front of his primitive house. Underfed and small in stature, he is not deterred by the absence of toys and even the limitation of space. He has started out on a trip of his own close to the building for a great adventure.

46

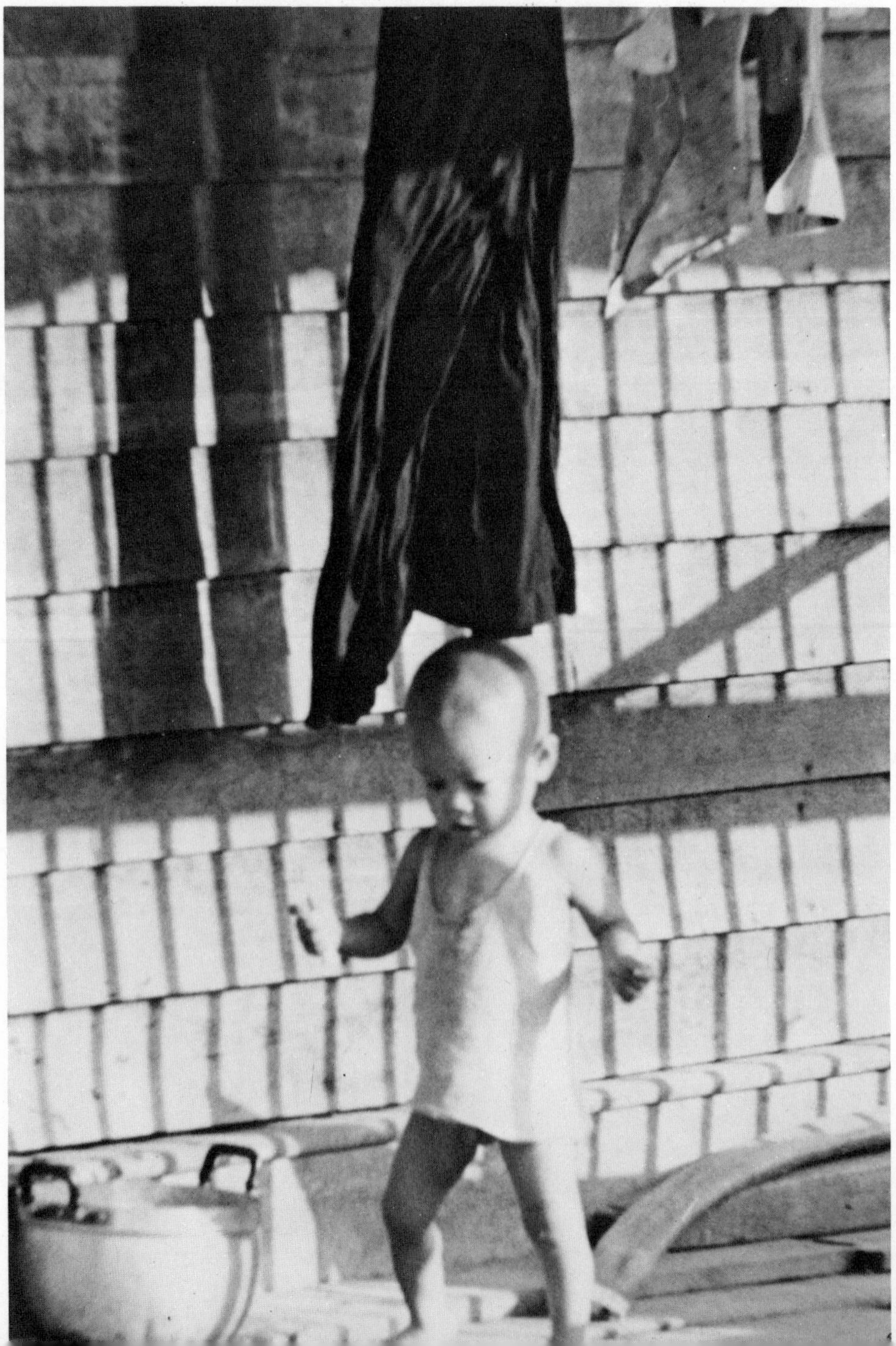

PHOTOGRAPH 47 was taken in a village in the Philippines, near a primitive abode. Three boys manage to have a grand time with—well, nearly nothing. Old cans are used to play "barter," exchanging a small quantity of sand for another (in the West, children play "shop" with more "civilized" implements). The setup and the sanitation are not recommended for child rearing, but the scene certainly demonstrates that children, under multifarious circumstances, do not need the paraphernalia of affluence to enjoy themselves. I have seen a four-year-old girl in a very deprived home amuse herself with a piece of string which she visualized as a giant, a bear, a good mother, a bad mother, an angry father, embroidering with this thin thread yards and yards of fantasy.

47

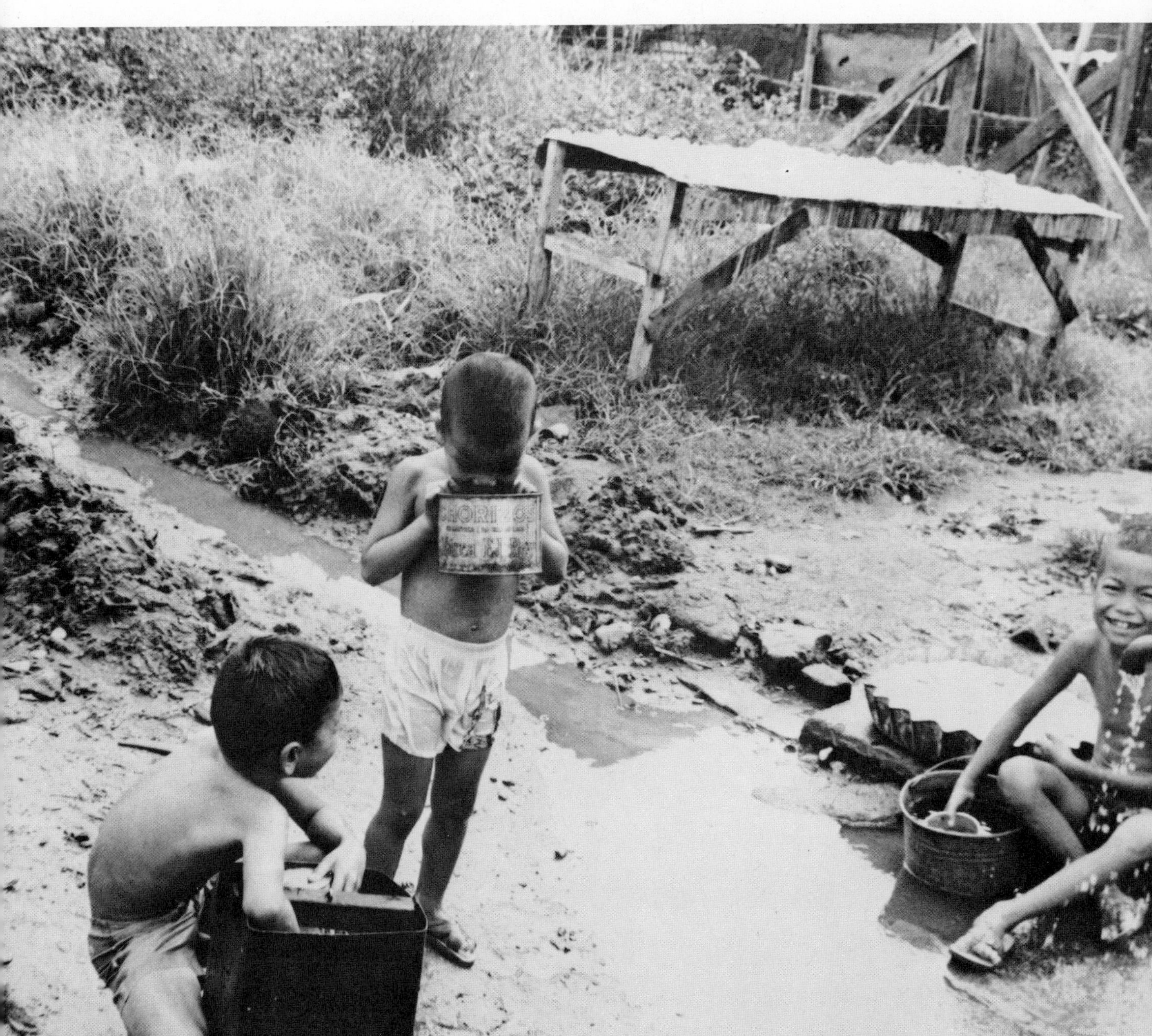

10

The joy of eating

> . . . if I eat *well,* I am congratulated; my grandmother herself cries out: "What a good boy to be so hungry!"
>
> JEAN-PAUL SARTRE, *The Words*

"Eating is for growing, that's what the grown-ups all the time say." But eating can also be fun. This is amply demonstrated by an instance I once observed on a transatlantic liner. It was breakfast time, and at a neighboring table I noticed a boy of about two-and-a-half sitting next to his mother. The mother was engaged in conversation with people at the table, but from time to time she would look toward her little boy and smile. This youngster was very busy; he had rejected a baby seat, his nose was just above his plate. He went through three pieces of buttered toast the way a plow goes systematically through a field. Then the waiter brought him a full-sized order of scrambled eggs. I expected the boy to pick up a spoon. Instead, with his right hand he took the fork near his plate and dug into the heap of eggs. Noticing that the semi-solid mass was overflowing on the outer edge of his fork, he started to bring his left index finger close to the plate, obviously intending to use it as a pusher; then he thought better of it and grabbed a man-size knife, put it parallel to the outer edge of the fork, tapping it lightly to align the overflow.

In this manner, he continued to eat the whole portion to the last scrap. At intervals he raised himself slightly, stretched out his arm and took a gulp or two of his milk. The whole performance was a masterpiece. Unfortunately, no cameraman was available, but I had called it to the attention of my tablemates. Although he was aware that we were watching him, he went through the whole meal quite unselfconsciously. I was intrigued by his behavior, which had no compulsive flavor and seemed so free of rigid training. He was eager and natural.

I made it my business to follow him later on deck and found him a sturdy, lively, sociable, conspicuously well-adjusted child. The deck was for him a racecourse and, in spots, an obstacle course. He was running the whole length of it, climbing or jumping over unoccupied deck chairs. From time to time he ran to his mother, bursting with joy and a sense of accomplishment, to recount his exploits. Although as unselfconscious as he had been in the dining room, he was also aware of people around him, especially the young ones, enticing some little children to join him in his play.

By chance, on the very same day at another table, there was a boy of approximately the same age, sitting on his mother's lap and causing great agitation around him. The mother was enumerating to him all the goodies, liquid and otherwise, that he could have for lunch. Would he take orange juice? "No, I want soup!" All other offers from the menu met with the same answer. He repeated automatically, "I want soup!" The mother's exasperation was visibly mounting and she finally settled with an order for the only soup that was available, an onion soup, which she had been sure he wouldn't like. When he saw the strange brown fluid in front of him, he took his spoon and slapped it on the surface, causing mini waterworks. "Not that one!" he bellowed. Tablemates did not

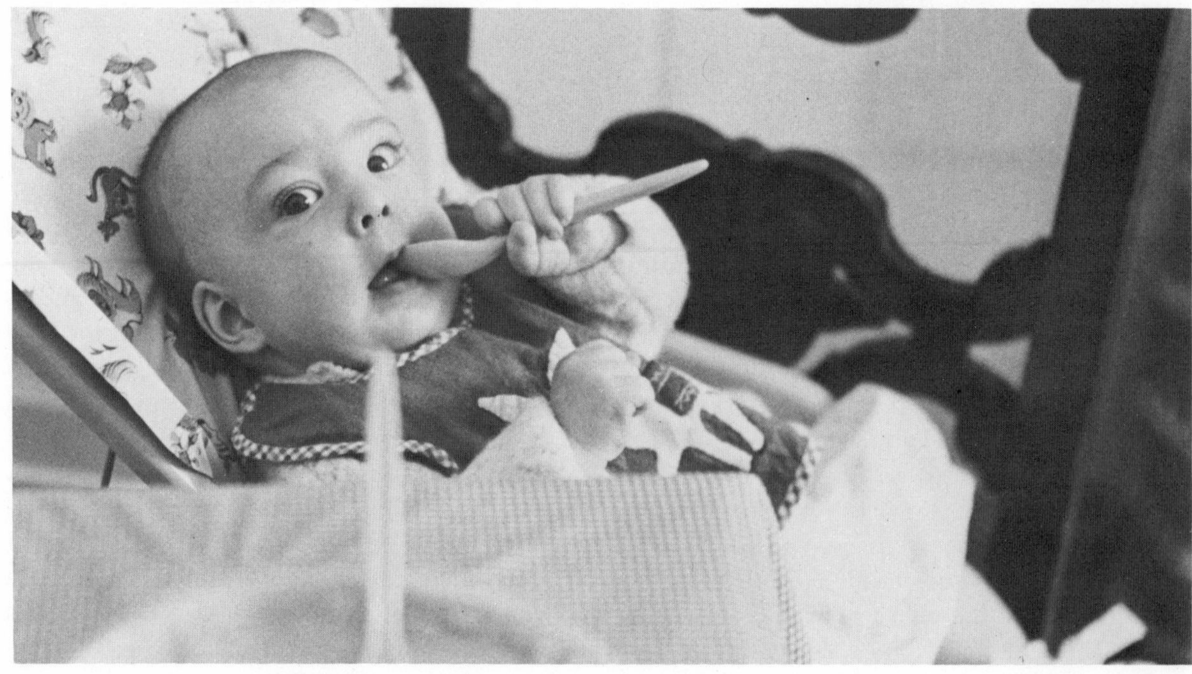

48

appreciate the general showering. By then, the mother was completely out of patience. She slapped his hand, causing a second display of waterworks, got up angrily and carried him from the table. The child swiftly grabbed a roll in passing—and that was his lunch. There was no difficulty in tracing this boy on deck; from great distances he could be heard whining, screaming, with the mother helpless before his display of temper. Multiple choices may be an approved method for testing scholastic knowledge, but in the young mind they create only confusion and a desire to escape or rebel.

49

A young child who is physically and emotionally healthy generally likes to eat. The physiological need is behind the appetite, so the grownups are right after all—"Eating is for growing." But there is more to it than that: for the young child, as we have seen earlier, *incorporation* (taking into the body), as a physical fact and as a symbol, is a primary need (hand to mouth). Feeding is also evidence of love from the dispenser, the mother as a rule. In addition it is a delight to the senses: the taste, the smell, the consistency. While the intellectual function is slowly unfolding, the senses are operating full force, providing the separate elements which are basic to observation and reasoning.

At six months, Sophia is enormously interested in food and the implements used in the handling of food. Having emptied her dish of baby food, she hangs on to the spoon which is her very own (PHOTOGRAPH 48); it is similar to the one her mother has used to feed her. She is a little surprised that a photographer should take an interest in her feeding. But why not? After all, eating is a great thing. This child, who is generally cheerful and interested in everything around her, takes a particular interest in her food. She has not been breast fed but she has accepted substitutes without resistance; her development has been normal. She is a smiling, wide-awake child and a very good feeder.

It is obvious that at three-and-a-half Sophia still relishes her food. The mother has had the good sense not to insist on cleanliness and care of the face, hands, or bib. When babies grab their food with their hands, you know that they love it. They don't need to be coaxed or cajoled into the scheme of "eating for growing." In PHOTOGRAPH 49, Sophia is seen to be eager to clean up every scrap of food in her bowl, her fingers carrying small particles deep into her mouth.

11

Just like Mommy, just like Daddy

A hundred little things make likenesses
In brethren born, and show the father's blood.

EURIPIDES, *Electra*

His whole picture of his father's world—the world in which his father moved—as he built it in his brain with all the naive but passionate intensity of childhood, was not unlike a Currier and Ives drawing, except that here the canvas was more crowded and the scale more large. It was a world that was drawn in very bright and very innocent and very thrilling colors.

THOMAS WOLFE, *The Web and the Rock*

In the past, it was thought that the child tries to *imitate* the parent of the same sex: a son, his father; a daughter, her mother. More recent knowledge of the mechanisms involved points to what is known as *identification* with the parent.

In PHOTOGRAPHS 50, 51, and 52 we see Sophia again. She has been caught by the photographer in one of her favorite activities, putting on her mother's clothing. There is more to this process than just imitating. It would be impossible for a child consciously to copy the posture, the gait, the facial expression, and the actions of the parent involved. What the child projects is a faithful image, in miniature, of that parent.

Sophia has put on her mother's shoes and carries her mother's handbag. The projection of the mother's image is true in every detail: the tilt of the head, the engaging smile, the friendliness, all are there to identify an adult, her mother. These pictures are by no means unusual. Halloween, for instance, is a favorite of children, especially girls, because it gives them the opportunity to play a part. Dress, makeup, gestures, and voices are borrowed from the adult world for one exciting night. Walking may be considerably hampered by the floor-length clothes, but even this is no serious handicap.

Without benefit of special occasions, Sophia frequently sneaks into her mother's room to take shoes, clothes, hats, and other accessories that stamp the mother in her own style. Sophia is very pleased with herself. For a brief interval, she IS her mother, which does not mean that she would give her mother's name as her own—she knows very well that her name remains Sophia. She may have no personal use for the bag but, at this moment, it is *her* bag. She finally encounters some difficulty and must acknowledge that she is only Sophia, not her mother, when she decides to start out on a walk with all this apparel. Oversized shoes are a little clumsy, but she must step down. Have no fear. She does.

This identification process is one of the forms in which the desire to grow into an adult manifests itself. The young child's life proceeds in an alternating rhythm, forward and backward. Sophia cannot wait to become a "real grownup" and she has fleeting illusions that she is one—specifically, her mother. In succeeding moments she may show infantile behavior such as thumbsucking or whining, and this is not an abnormal pattern either. Emotional progress does not follow an arrow's course. A child could not sustain the thrust forward at an adult tempo, but the impetus of this thrust is necessary for growth. Parents are sometimes annoyed with this adventure in Time, failing to recall their own wishful thinking: a girl of thirteen, unveiling the fantasies that followed her first menstrual period, recalled that she rehearsed engagement, marriage, and childbirth in her own mind. Her daydreams revolved, in every detail, around adult bits of life.

50

51

52

In PHOTOGRAPHS 53 and 54, we have the same phenomenon enacted by a boy. This seven-year-old frequently adopts his father's walk. His hands behind his back or in his pockets, he walks as his father does, mulling ponderous thoughts. The walk is not a child's walk; he IS his father. It is a great comfort to him, this feeling that he can walk, talk, and behave as if he were his father. This brings the father down to an acceptable size.

A twelve-year-old boy had taken up the habit of jiggling small change in his pockets, a habit absorbed from his father who, both hands in his pockets, was continually playing with coins. One day, the boy was walking in a street near his home, as usual playing with his coins, when a group of slightly older boys approached him with an imperative, "Give the dough." He was frightened, and ran to a nearby stationery store, where his parents had an account. He lingered there for a while, hoping he had dropped "the enemy." However, when he came out, this time omitting the jingle, he found the same gang. Since he had revealed his wealth, it could not be denied. However, he was also knowledgeable in what his parents called "foul language"; on this particular occasion the knowledge came in very handy. He reeled off an obscene sentence about his assailants' brains; they responded with approval and a comment that "He is one of us" and left him alone. They had obviously taken him for the son of a rich man (which he indeed was). The identification with the father had proved only too faithful, but the street language learned despite parental disapproval had served him in good stead.

A differentiation has been made between imitation and identification: identification is, on an unconscious basis, a strong drive to *be* one's parent, whereas imitation implies the conscious effort to be and do *like* one's parent. In imitative behavior, there is a substratum of identification drive.

53

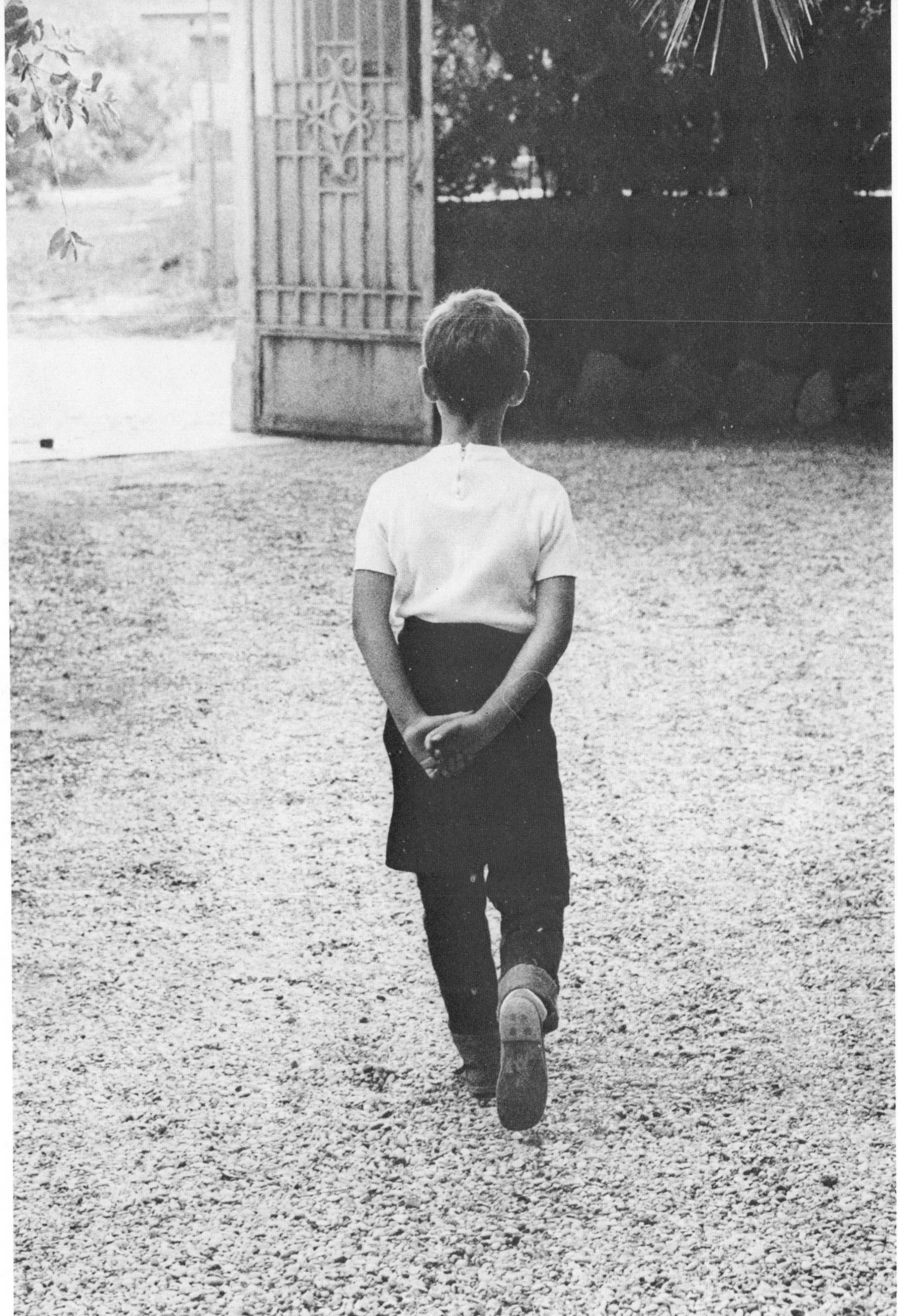

54

In the next photographs, we were fortunate to catch a boy-father relationship which exemplifies the admixture of imitation and identification. Donny, three years old, has a new little sister who, quite as expected, monopolizes his mother's attention. He has become the shadow of his young father in all activities. In PHOTOGRAPHS 55, 56, 57, and 58, we see him getting ready to do what his father does every morning, get shaved. So, every day, he too "shaves." His parents have bought him a toy razor which he uses with great skill (all

55

56

the gestures are there) and, in his own mind, with very satisfactory results even if no hair is available for removal. He studies the different steps of his father's procedure. You see him watching in the mirror as his father lathers his chin, which he later imitates accurately. The application of shaving cream, with a generous reaching out to just under the eyes, faithfully follows the father's technique. There is no doubt in his mind that he is, himself, just like Daddy, shaving.

Another favorite occupation is "reading"

57

58

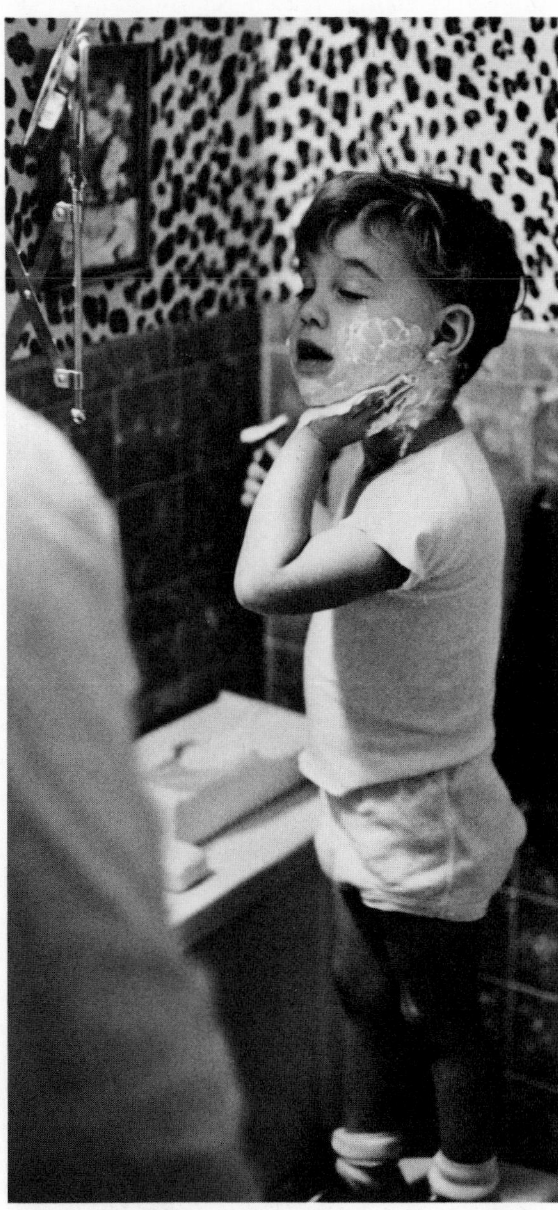

his father's newspaper. We see him in PHOTOGRAPHS 59 and 60 handling with great skill two advertising sections of *The New York Times,* in which his father for the moment shows no interest. Perchance he "reads" them straight up, not upside down, but this must be a matter of luck. Judging from his presence and posture in PHOTOGRAPH 59, one would think our young "reader" considerably older than three.

To young children, reading is one of the most puzzling of adult activities. For a few years after they have started "reading," children nurture the gratifying thought that they really can read. Only the grownups don't recognize their talents. They think reading is a grownup privilege. Being read to can be so frustrating, but it is also a bit of a compensation to detect deficiencies in the adult omniscience. If a word is omitted or misread, children are quick to call attention to the adult's gross mishandling of the text. Sometimes they are even able to point to the exact spot where that word belongs, having many times followed, not the text to be sure, but the word-images, and linked them with their corresponding phonetics.

However, it is a rude awakening to discover that, left to one's own devices, one finds the printed page quite lacking in eloquence. A charming story, which I know to be written in at least four languages (French, Italian, German, and Russian), runs as follows: A grandmother, her steel-frame glasses on, reads a story to her grandson. He follows with fascinated attention, but the grandmother at one point must interrupt her reading; she leaves book and glasses on the table. The little boy,

59

enthralled by the story, cannot wait till Grandma returns; suddenly, he decides that perhaps he could go on with it; he takes the book upside down, then right side up; he is thoroughly disappointed, seeing not a story but a mass of black and white squiggles. Perhaps the reading glasses have something to do with being able to read, so he tries the glasses on his nose. *"Mais, bernique, où donc est l'histoire?" Il ne voit rien que noir et blanc.* ("Fiddlesticks, where is the story?" He sees nothing but black and white.)

The writing process is at first even more mysterious. A child "writes" (i.e., scribbles), and having covered a page with hieroglyphics in what he thinks is the style of an older sibling's script, he asks, "What does it say?" If told that since *he* wrote it, perhaps he could tell what it says, he is not about to lose face, and immediately produces a text. A three-year-old boy attending nursery school, confronted with such a question, reels off: "A nice president (vice-president) in Washington and a bad wolf shows his big teeth, I'm going to eat you up (looking anxious) and you know what? Michael (his friend at nursery school) got on the steps of my big building and it fell down (now angry)." A bit of current events, a fragment of nightmare, a foreshortened actual experience, helter-skelter, he too has "written" a story and is very pleased with the results.

Donny's "reading" technique is impeccable. In PHOTOGRAPH 60 we see him discarding a section of the paper. This is indeed a distinctly adult gesture and the little fellow is surely convinced that he is through reading the section.

60

Where Donny really shines as almost a replica of his father is seen in PHOTOGRAPHS 61, 62, and 63. His bed needs to be repaired; one caster has come off, making the bed unsteady. Father and son are engaged in what seems to be a professional job. They are on the floor with two hammers, one the father's and the other Donny's. When Donny discovers a flat disc he thinks is the missing caster he is jubilant. "Is that the one?" is clearly legible on his face. This is a red-letter day; he feels as big and important as his father.

In some cases, we find a boy who identifies for too long a time with his mother. (In the first year, this is normal and necessary for the baby of either sex.) At the very beginning of his life, the male infant, who has been a part of his mother for nine months, remains very dependent upon her. He may smile at his father who jiggles something in front of him,

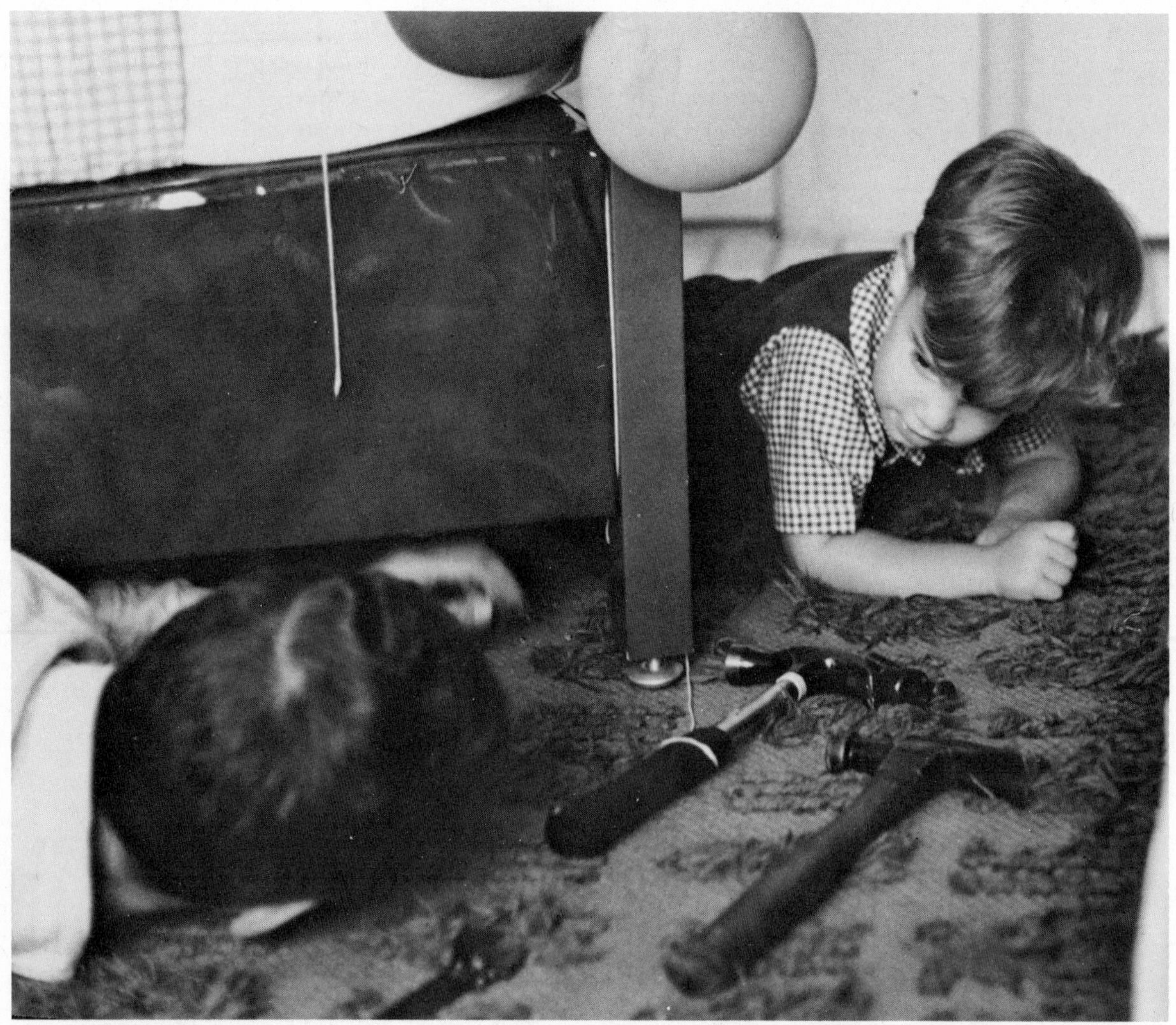

61

but his dependence on and attachment to his mother are of prime importance. It is a condition for survival. By the age of two, when he has become to an extent physically independent, his world widens. Prolonged dependence on the mother spells difficulties in later years. The mother who encourages her son to remain an infant makes it difficult for him to move on to the next state, and such a mother has helped create the "mama's boy."

We can be assured that Donny and his young father are so attuned that there is no danger of his becoming "mama's boy." Obviously, the father in this case is quite capable of giving of himself and shows no impatience toward the shadow at his side. He was the one to suggest a toy razor and to accept an unskilled collaborator in carpentry, mechanics, and other household jobs. No defeat for this child in his male identification.

62

63

12

Curiosity revisited

> I have seen
> A curious child, who dwelt upon a tract
> Of inland ground, applying to his ear
> The convolutions of a smooth-lipped shell,
> To which, in silence hushed, his very soul
> Listened intensely; and his countenance soon
> Brightened with joy, for from within were heard
> Murmurings, whereby the monitor expressed
> Mysterious union with its native sea.
>
> WILLIAM WORDSWORTH, *The Excursion*

In our earlier acquaintance with the curiosity of young children (Chapter 4), we were dealing with the intense drive in children to see what is around them and to find some explanations of their own about the relations between people, between people and objects, and between objects—a true manifestation of the scientific spirit.

Another aspect of the curiosity of young children relates to finding satisfactory answers to questions that they seldom bring to the attention of adults or that they feel will not be answered. There is, for instance, what might be called "the mystery of the closed door." Children are fully aware that something goes on between parents which is either withheld from them or met with evasion when they ask a question directly. An experiment carried out at the Payne Whitney Nursery School with a view to studying personality development in young children included a certain family-play situation. The children were provided with dolls as human symbols: a man, a woman, and two children (a baby and a young child of the same sex as the child being observed). Beds were also available, and bedtime was a favorite subject for play-acting. Frequently expressed was curiosity regarding the fact that parents are "in pairs" and "I am always alone."

64

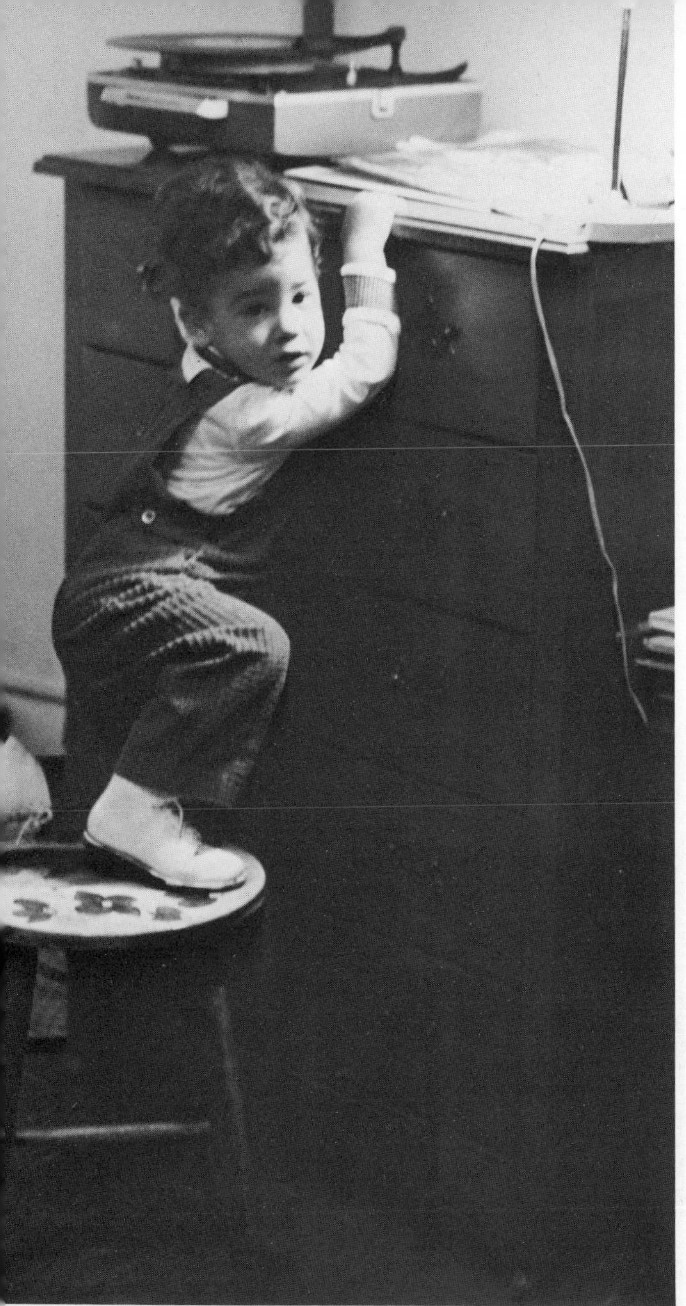

65

In PHOTOGRAPH 64, two-year-old Dennis is in the process of opening a door, for his age a physical feat convincingly projected in the picture. This is his parents' bedroom. It is daytime and no one is there, but—*well, a door must be opened. What is behind a door? What is in the clothes closet? Well, clothes, of course. But in the corners, on the floor, on the shelves? What else? What is in that box, on that chest? And all those kitchen pots and pans, pull them out of the cabinet—the grownups don't understand—the fun is to pull them out, one by one, and spread them on the floor. The grownups only want them on the stove, but the stove! Ah! No, no!*

Dennis is curious about what is behind the door, although he has seen it many times. He has been curious about everything, within reach and out of reach, since he learned to walk, over a year ago. In PHOTOGRAPH 65 we see him at the peak of his investigating power as he climbs a high stool to reach the record player on the dresser. His parents may have been a little leery at first, but a few mishaps were not enough to discourage Dennis, as we can see in his skillful handling of the record player in PHOTOGRAPH 66. This is an unusually advanced child. His parents gave him freedom early and no one is going to stop him from investigating what at any given moment moves him.

66

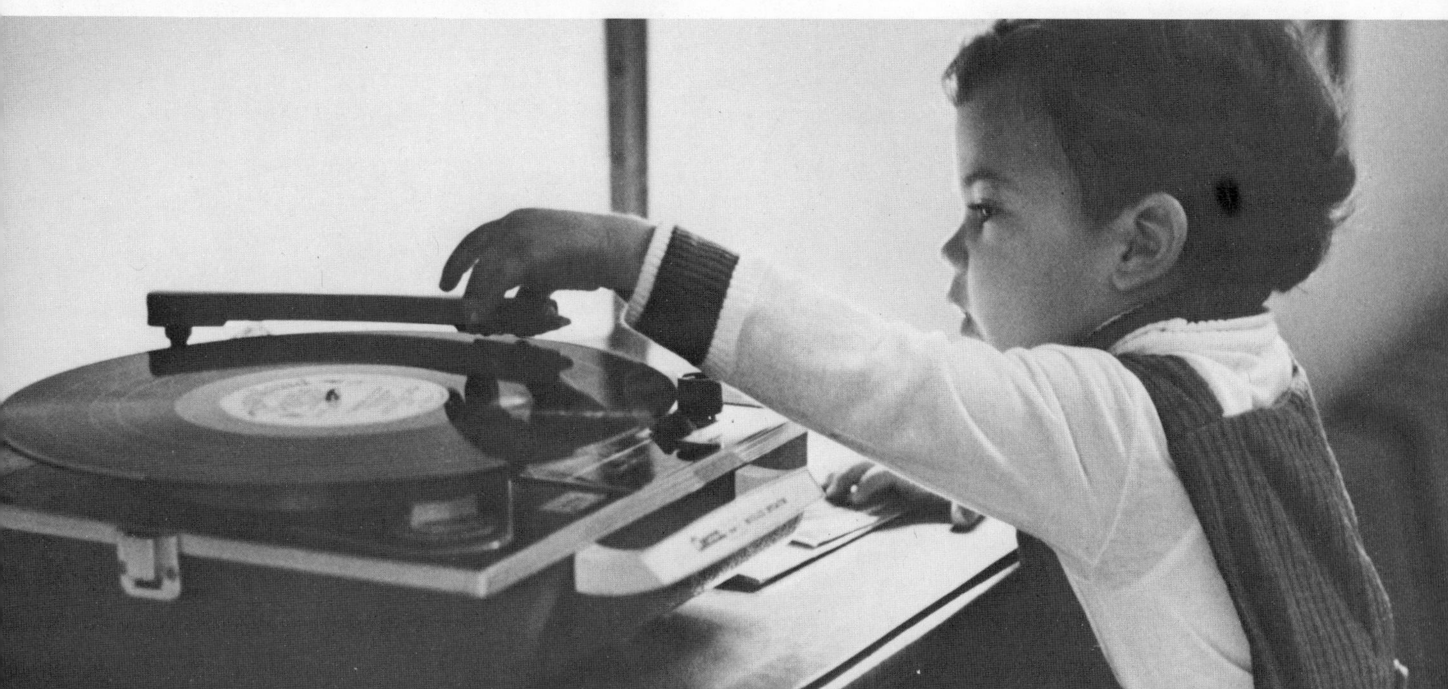

The two boys in PHOTOGRAPH 67 are considerably older, ten and eleven years respectively. They have found a rubber raft and started on a sea voyage. There is nothing but water all around them. They are already some distance from the shore, with no provisions for a long trip and only the sun as a companion, but away they go; at least they cherish the idea that, with hard rowing, they'll get ahead. Besides, they can swim, so if the boat turns over, they can do their act. Nothing to worry about. Who is going to say that it is dangerous to start on an ocean trip in a lifeboat? They know that, of course, but is there a grownup around to remind them? The only audible voice now is the inner voice.

One cannot help but think of the imaginative fable projected in a recent Czechoslovak film, *The Seventh Continent*. A boy and a girl, who are accompanying their parents on a small boat, start out on a minor search for the girl's basket, which has fallen overboard. It is at

67

this point that the fable begins: a rubber raft conveniently appears and the two children launch their fanciful voyage. The trip takes on gigantic proportions when children from all over the world join them. Maps materialize from nowhere and the children create islands and continents from their images. Drawings of palm trees burst out into living trees with coconuts ready to eat—from the abstract to the concrete, a mental process truly childlike; a child's paradise of pure imagination. The children are uninhibited in their criticisms of the elders' society. This film in its entirety is an orchestration of the inner voices of children.

Wide-open spaces with unlimited sea water are not always available. Then, how to fantasy adventure and mystery? In PHOTOGRAPH 68, a six-year-old boy, who has been told by his pals that there is an exciting tunnel not too far from where he lives, starts out on the road to the unknown; his two-wheeler, though of minimal size, is fully equipped with shiny mechanical parts, brakes, lights, horn. The owner of such a vehicle exudes prestige. However, now that he is facing the opening of the tunnel, he feels frightened. Putting the bicycle aside, he starts on a reconnoitering escalation, hoping that perhaps sounds outside of the tunnel will give useful information. There might be dangerous animals, a mad dog, a wild cat, some rats, a snake; one's imagination runs away with one. He is attempting to get to the top of the tunnel on the outside, the way a physician starts with the auscultation of lungs and heart of his patient. Who knows, maybe the big kids are hidden somewhere in the tunnel to scare him stiff. Having started full of ambition, he is now stalled in what promised to be a great adventure. It is not even certain that he will pedal through the tunnel, the inner voices are so tumultuous at this instant.

68

69

Living in New York City offers neither limitless water nor mysterious terrain to exploit. In PHOTOGRAPH 69 we have a beautiful demonstration of on-the-spot curiosity. Three friends (the two youngest are brothers) have been roaming in a shabby street on the lookout for anything of interest. The two older boys have found a sheet of paper, a discarded letter, and they pore over it with intense curiosity. Even the ball is forgotten. The middle boy, hugging his ball closely, is very intent on deciphering a message which can have little meaning to him but appears more readable than his textbooks of arithmetic or language arts. Those are really boring. At the moment, to know "What could there be on that page?" seems of capital importance.

The brother of the ballplayer is going home with a trophy. He will beg for time and may be allowed to use his find for a few hours before Mother insists it must be discarded as not safe, not clean, and for a lot of other grownup reasons. Meanwhile his pride in carrying that broken-down rocker gives him the air of the leader of a triumphal march. How Mother will greet him at the end of that march doesn't concern him for the moment.

So even a New York street offers opportunities. City children do not feel the lack of contact with nature until they have been exposed to it. I recall a nine-year-old boy seen at the clinic who had left New York for the first time on a two-week camping trip. When he returned, he tried to communicate the feeling of exultation he had experienced walking barefoot in the morning on the wet grass. I could not convince him that I understood his feeling. He repeated obstinately, "No, you don't know what it is to walk in the wet soft grass after those hard streets of New York."

In PHOTOGRAPH 70, a little girl, alone in the street, is full of joy at the possession of a piece of loot she has picked up, probably in a garbage can. It is somewhat fancy, with a lace effect. She is running home to make use of the prize. Children are great collectors, even if they are also great "destroyers." The inner voices are not always working in unison.

70

13

There are also the others

Far from wanting to shine, I laughed in chorus with the others, I repeated their catchwords and phrases, I kept quiet, I obeyed, I imitated my neighbors' gestures, I had only one desire: to be integrated.

JEAN-PAUL SARTRE, *The Words*

As we have seen earlier, very young children are, through sheer necessity, the epitome of egocentrism. They think of themselves, their needs, the satisfactions and love they receive from their environment, the physical pain or disappointments they may experience. A closeness of individual-to-individual relation begins with the special attachment of the baby to its mother. This is gradually extended to the father and other members of the family. We have already seen an intrafamily relationship in Chapter 6.

In PHOTOGRAPHS 71, 72, and 73, we follow a brief episode in the life of a small family segment: a boy, six years old, his sister, three, and his younger brother, two. They are variously sitting, standing, crouching, all close by a bench in the park. The older boy is in charge. The first picture shows him quite detached from his job. He is, in fact, a little bored with the idea of watching his siblings and particularly the young brother. He longs for some activity away from the younger ones. His friends are at the other end of the park, busy with a game of catch. Nevertheless, there is an undercurrent of watchfulness, and when the little brother attempts to climb over the bench back, big brother is right there, his tense facial expression indicating his anxiety about the anticipated climb.

The left hand is ready to act in case of danger. He may not be an enthusiastic guardian of his brother and sister, but certainly he is a responsible one.

Meanwhile, little sister is left out by the two brothers. Being a girl between two boys is seldom an enviable position. She sees her opportunity to shoot it out and grabs the toy gun that belongs to the younger boy. Not much experience with that weapon. Awkwardly, she shoots at the clouds, rather pleased with herself. This is her one opportunity to be like the brothers. Such an opportunity does not come too often. The brothers are a closed corporation.

The spontaneous warmth of relations be-

71

72

73

tween children who, a short while before, were total strangers, is illustrated in PHOTOGRAPHS 74 and 75. The pictures were taken at a specialized clinic of the Presbyterian Hospital. The children have not even met (nobody is introducing anybody) but "What's your name" goes around. The name is quickly forgotten anyway, if registered at all. The drawing materials speak for themselves and all the children feel at home at the table; they choose crayons, pencils, paper, to suit their wishes. The eight-year-old boy, serious and organized, is at work on a composition of his choice; he has aroused attention and a touch of admiration from the left flank: two sisters, six and four-and-a-half years old,

74

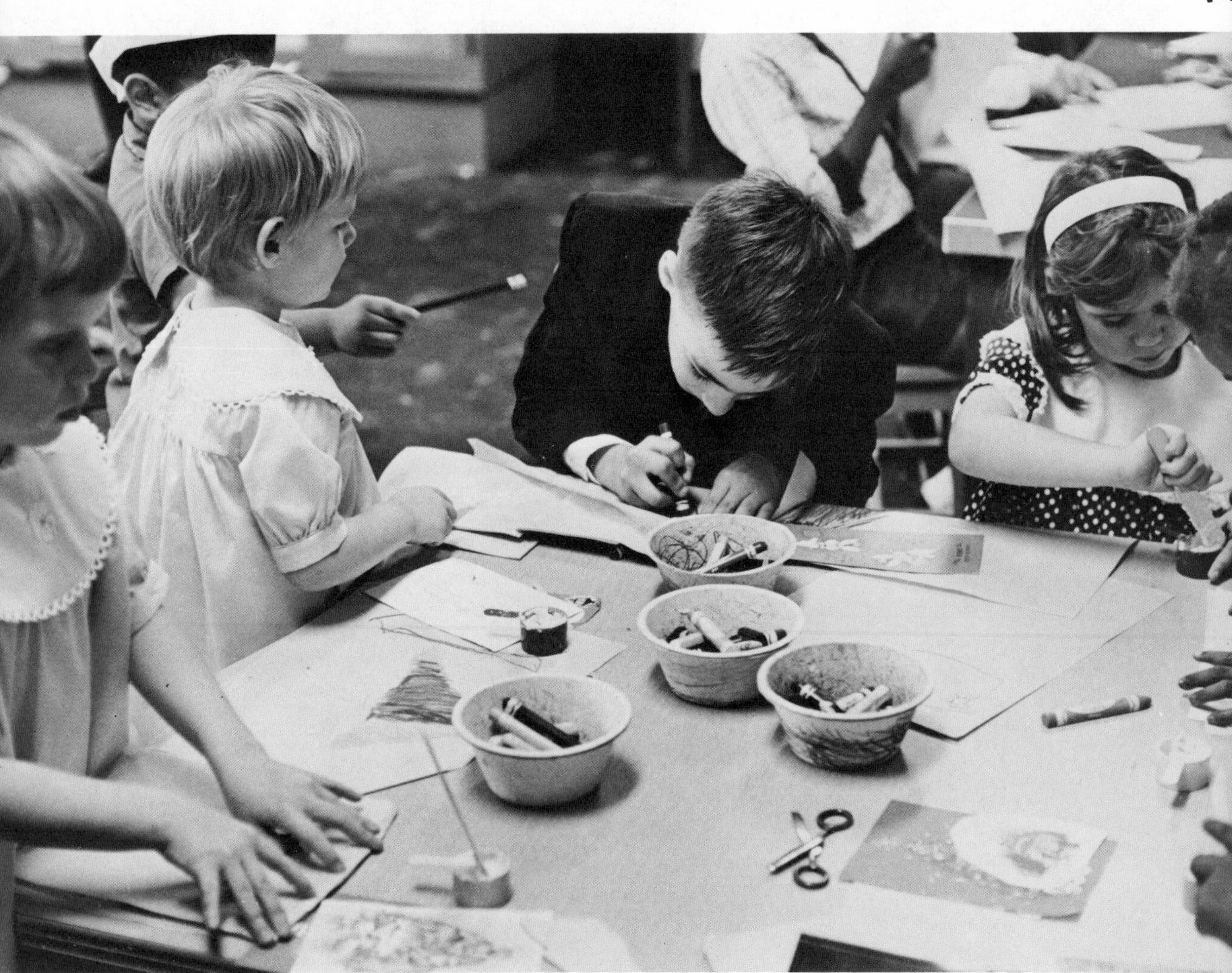

who have not yet worked out their own ideas, and the five-year-old boy, at first not visible, whose pencil points to the earnest artist. Each child follows his or her inclination; the hands at the right are very busy. There is a great fluidity in the relations between the children, each occupied with his or her self-designated task and yet each an integral part of the group. In PHOTOGRAPH 75, the five-year-old boy, last to arrive, has settled down on a corner seat. He does not seem too eager to start on any art production. Rather, he seems dazzled by his blond neighbor. The general's hat gives confidence in oneself. Who said that love at first sight awaits the adolescent years to put in its appearance?

75

14

Discovering one's body

Love's mysteries in souls do grow,
But yet the body is his book . . .
JOHN DONNE, *The Ecstasy*

When babies discover, very early, that their fingers are not separate objects coming into view but are parts of their own body, the subjective experience is one of surprise and pleasure. Many body sensations are also registered with delight; others puzzle and can even frighten them.

We have seen eighteen-month-old Adam exercising his body above and around the toilet seat just for fun—training could wait. (Even though he took bowel training very lightly success came to him effortlessly shortly after the pictures were taken.) In PHOTOGRAPH 76, he is waiting for Mother to get ready for some toilet procedure, before sleeping time. Apparently even waiting can be fun for Adam. He is waiting with amused tolerance. Take your time, Mother. No rush. Diversion is at hand. In PHOTOGRAPH 77 he discovers his penis, lingers over the stimulus and pleasurable sensation. It would be more accurate to say he rediscovers his penis; this he does at intervals, always with the same sense of novelty and satisfaction. It is as natural as was the pleasure of a nursing bottle after one had voiced, then satisfied, hunger. To Adam, the area is not out of bounds. His parents, anything but Victorians, have not

76

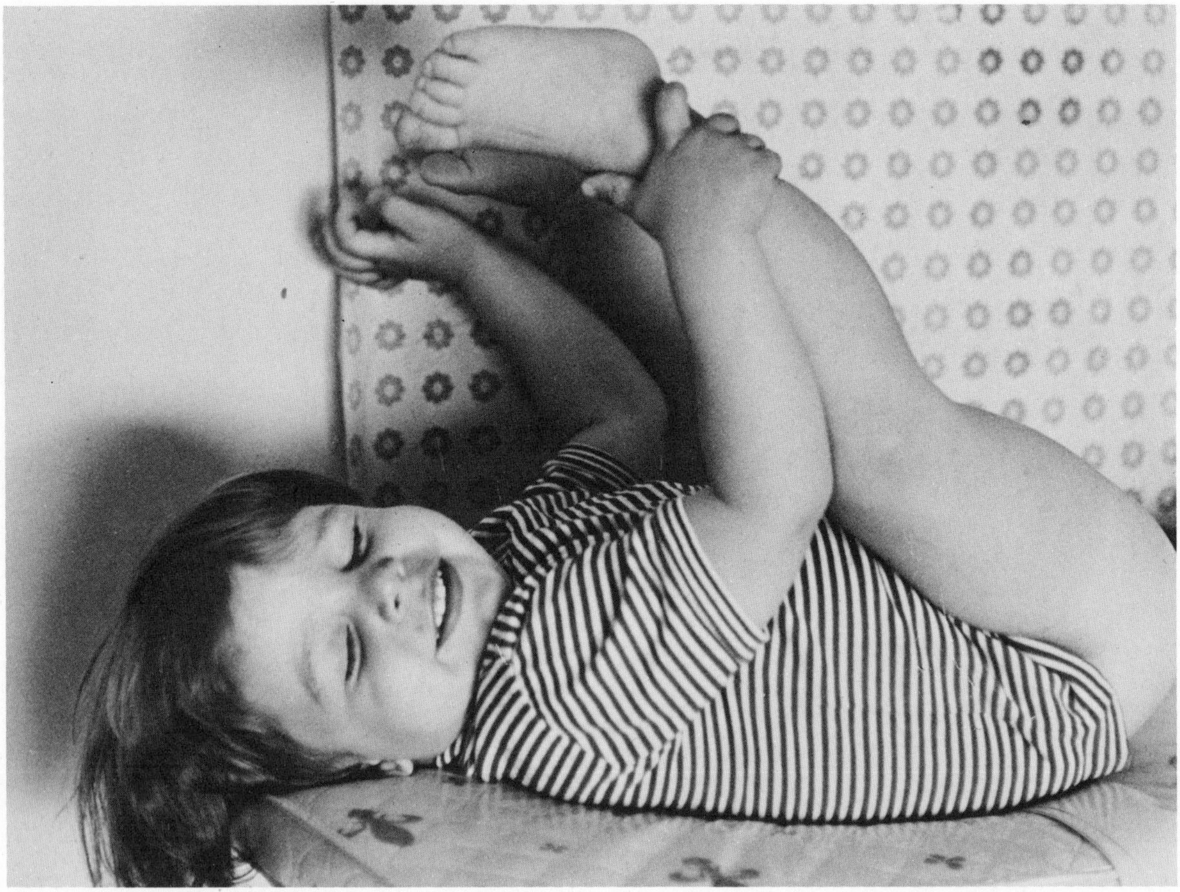

77

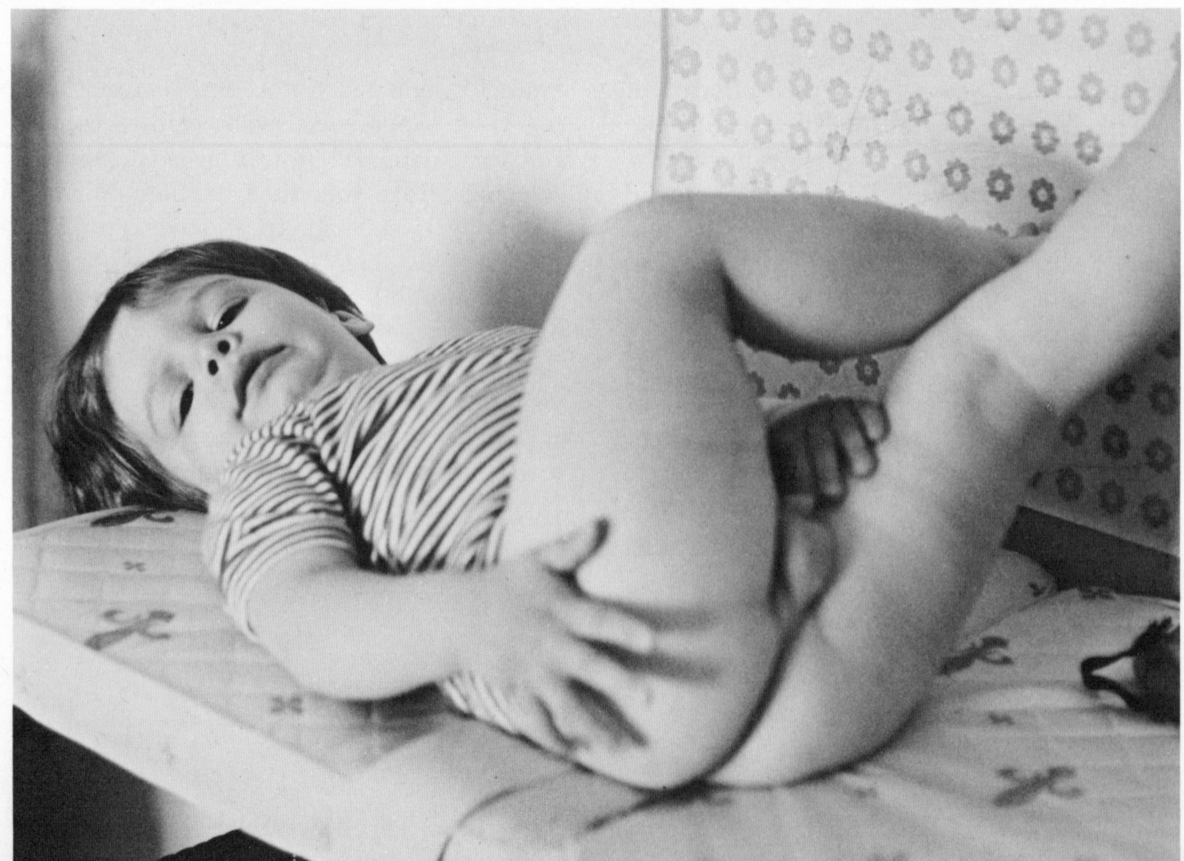

78

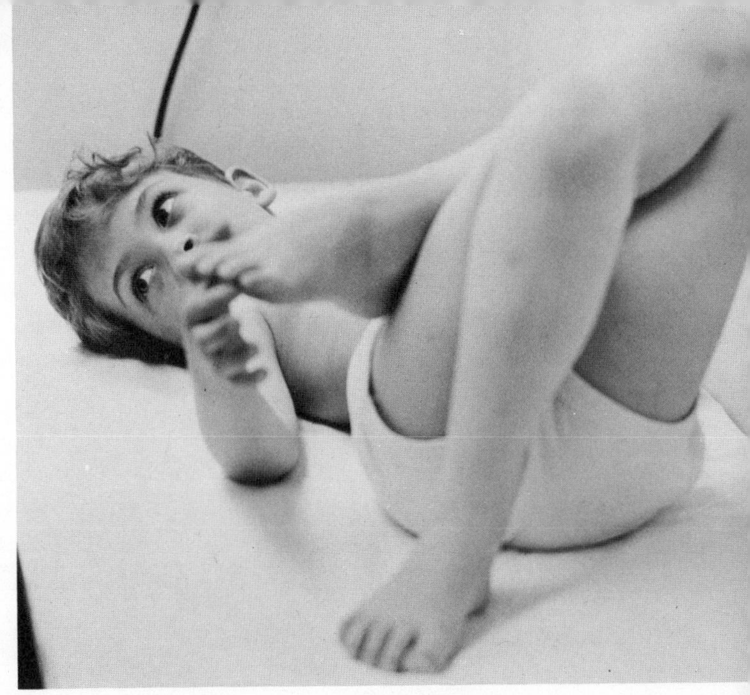

initiated the taboo which tends to create neurotic conflicts, so he has no sense of guilt about a gesture which in the not-too-distant past was repressed, more or less severely, with coaxing, threatening, and disciplining.

As young children develop, their interests expand, their human contacts and play activities multiply, and erotic stimulation is of lesser significance—until puberty, when physical and emotional changes take place and sexual urges appear. If children are excessively absorbed in their genitals, withdrawn from emotional involvement and from usual children's activities, it is not scolding they need, but the attention of a psychiatrist.

The interest in one's body lessens in proportion as outside interests increase. There are, however, certain circumstances which favor the return of earlier patterns of behavior. This type of regression is normally encountered in the course of physical illness. The seven-year-old boy in PHOTOGRAPH 78 is waiting in the Payne Whitney Clinic for a follow-up examination after serious abdominal surgery. Ordinarily, his feet would be of no special interest to him, but now he has been looking at them intently, biting the toenails, picking the skin around them. This is a regression which is evidence of his anxiety and diminished physical state. The accompanying adult apparently did not approve of this regression. Now, as is evident in PHOTOGRAPH 79, the child looks very subdued. He had found comfort out of his body; nailbiting, thumbsucking, are likely to return with physical illness. It is unfortunate that this adult could not understand the mechanism of regression. *Look at her! She is angry at me. Why? It felt so much better in my tummy —now it's starting again, that pain like something biting me inside! I wish the doctor would tell her it's O.K. Well, maybe it doesn't look so good, but if it makes you feel better. . . .*

79

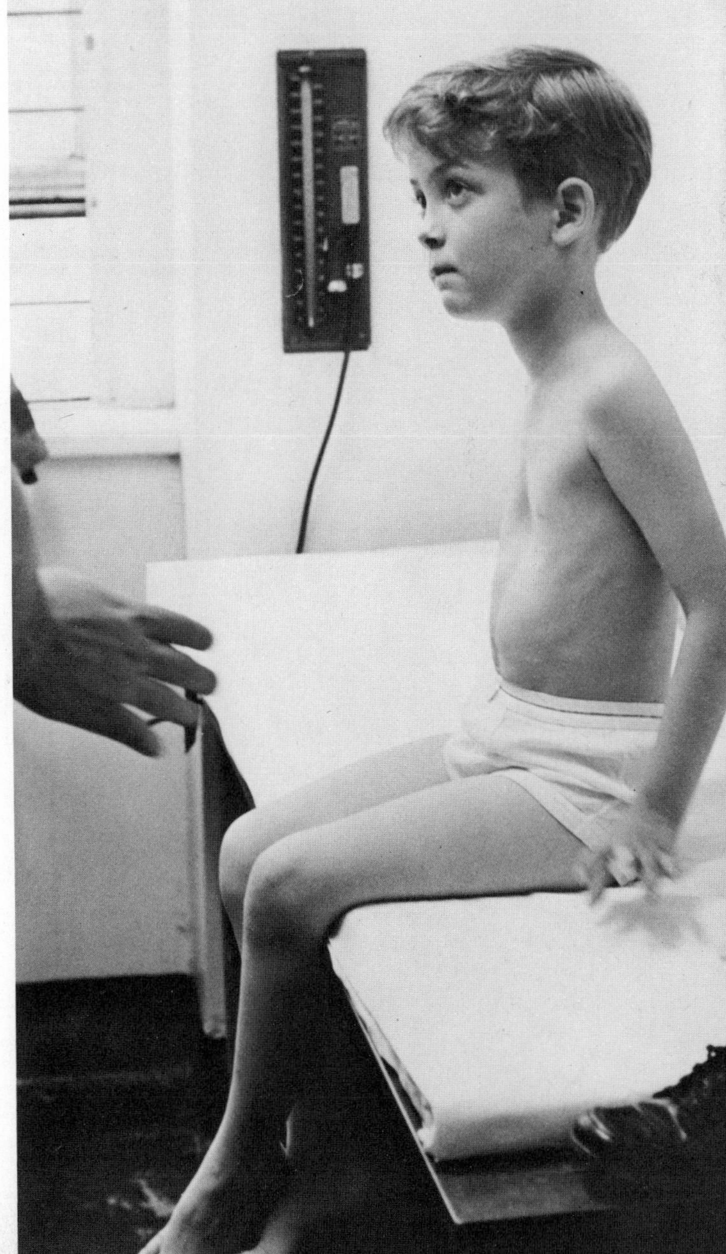

15

Why can't I have a pet?

> I think I could turn and live with animals . . . they are so placid and self-contain'd . . .
>
> WALT WHITMAN, *Song of Myself*

Children without siblings are likely to hound their parents for a pet. They are lonely, they want companionship; even if they have friends, these are not always available. Parents are familiar indeed with the repeated requests and harassing complaints about being "all by myself." A pet is the answer for the only child. A pet is amenable to training (though not always), never talks back, has no suggestions to offer on how to behave, and is more responsive than the adults around—in short, an ideal companion.

Children as a rule prefer a dog, then a cat, a hamster, even a rat or a mouse, but will settle for cold-blooded animals such as lizards, turtles, goldfish, if the closer-to-human animals are not permitted. Allergies in the family, concern about possible destruction and slovenliness, are usual motives for rejection (that is, rejection by the parents, not the child). No matter what the species, the child will endow the pet with all manner of human qualities, talk to it, confide in it, and be very possessive of it.

However distant the pet is from the human species, the child is equally involved, even if the relationship brings feebler returns. When the animal dies, a child can be just as troubled over a turtle as over a dog. An eight-year-old boy, an only child, enormously at-

80

tached to his turtle, lost it through a mishap for which he may have felt guilty although it is not certain that he had been negligent. The turtle was left in a small tank on the window sill, with the window open. Suddenly, the boy realized that his turtle was gone, and his distress was intense. Indeed he reverted to being a baby, climbed on his mother's lap and cried his grief out. This cold-blooded animal was to him a companion, and he could not bear its loss. He was insistent that the turtle should be brought back, ran down eight flights, and brought up the bloody mass. He also insisted on giving it a "formal" burial and found a spot in the park for that purpose.

In PHOTOGRAPHS 80, 81, and 82, we again find four-and-a-half-year-old Sophia. Sophia is an only child. Her parents are separated, and she has moments of acute loneliness. She cherishes her large, long-haired dog. Don't

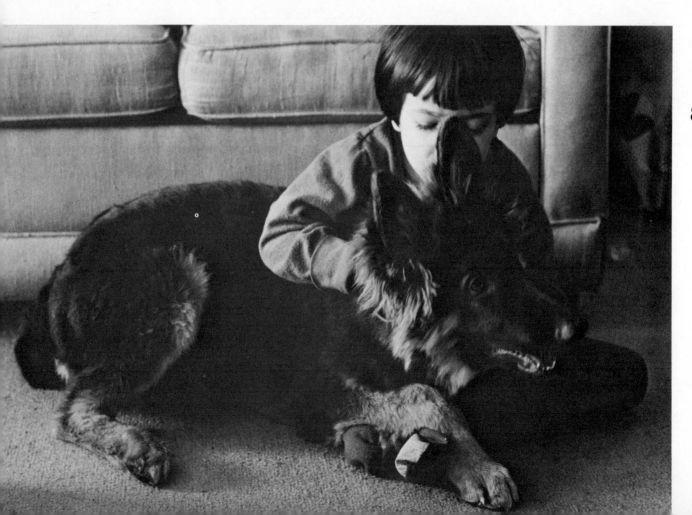

81

ask about pedigree. What is that? To Sophia, he is just a dog, a nice one. She spends a great deal of time with him, romping on the floor. The dog, though boisterous, is always gentle. He sleeps close by and she has a great feeling of security, even at night alone in her room when active games are at an end. She confides all her secrets to him. She has many secrets to communicate. *Why did Daddy leave? Will he ever come back? Maybe because I was naughty, that's why. Maybe he likes that other lady better. Maybe he will marry her. You know, my doggie, that I love you. I know you wouldn't leave me.* When the dog becomes a little too effusive, as in PHOTOGRAPH 82, she only raises her hand in front of her face in a not too convincing protective gesture. With this pet of hers she knows only happy times, and his companionship makes up in part for what she feels she is missing.

Of course, the only child does not have a monopoly over the insistent wish for a pet. In a large family a zoo will soon accumulate: a large variety of specimens from bird to fish, and a small mammal or two. Family life can be complicated by the rivalries resulting from multiple-pet ownership. Obviously, pets are not all blessings to parents. Children start out with considerable enthusiasm about their pet. They will train it, they will wash it, they will feed it, they will walk it—but after a period of two or three weeks the enthusiasm may wane. The children still want their companion but find the chores a burden which eventually falls upon Mother, naturally.

I recall a family with two children, a girl of twelve and a boy of ten. The sibling relationship was not fully satisfactory and each child insisted on having a separate pet. The girl wanted a long-haired dog and the boy, a short-haired one. Both dogs were to be large.

82

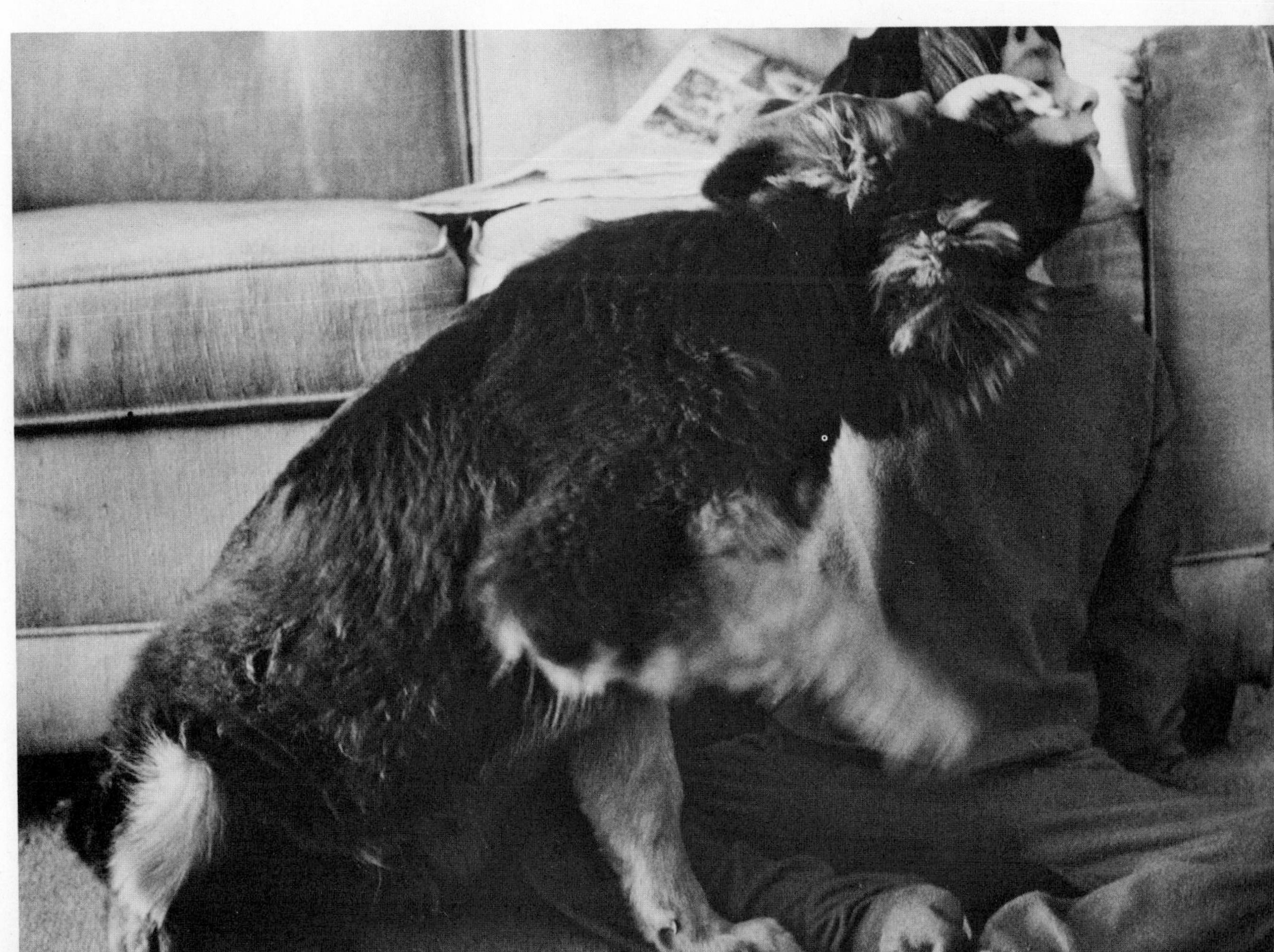

A compromise in the shape of one dog of medium size with a reasonably long coat was rejected. After much family palaver, the parents bought a collie for the girl and a boxer for the boy. At this point, the household became very lively. The dogs did not get along too well together—possibly reflecting the emotional attitudes of their young masters. They had to be fed and walked separately. It was not long before the exasperated mother, having inherited both, got rid of her cumbersome house-guests.

16

Physical pain and body sensations

When one's all right, he's prone to spite
The doctor's peaceful mission;
But when he's sick, it's loud and quick
He bawls for a physician.

EUGENE FIELD, *Doctors*

Is not short payne well borne, that bringes long ease. . . . ?

EDMUND SPENSER, *The Faerie Queene*

Many of our photographs were taken at the outpatient department of the Payne Whitney Clinic. This afforded an opportunity to observe and record the reactions of children to physical pain and other body sensations. These reactions showed great variations, as could be expected. We know some children who look forward to their visit to the doctor's office (a lollipop, a magic ring—of regal plastic—can help), but there are also the children for whom the equivalent reflex-like response to "doctor" is SHOTS. At the clinic, a truly democratic spirit prevails: no lollipop, no magic ring, but drawing materials are available for all who wish to use them; temperature taking and blood examination are distributed without any touch of favoritism, and there is comfort in the universality of the approach. One child who has just arrived watches another with a thermometer in the same place he's later going to have it. The young patients are familiar with the routine.

In PHOTOGRAPHS 83, 84, and 85, we see a fifteen-month-old boy whose rectal temperature is being taken by his mother (the nurse has thought very sensibly that a familiar hand might be more readily accepted)—no shots, yet the howl is practically audible. *Help! Murder!* Mother is gentle, but determined, and Sonny knows that there is no way to escape. He is expecting the worst, despite previous similar experiences and Mother's soft words of reassurance. *Mommy doesn't understand the scare, that pointed thing inside! I don't want it! Quick! Someone pull it out! Something awful is going to happen!* This fear that "something awful is going to happen" is by no means a rare feeling. Anything that may be felt as a threat to the body integrity, particularly in connection with the orifices—enema, ear cleaning, temperature taking, mouth inspection—can cause anxiety in a young child. This is especially true of the rectal and genital areas.

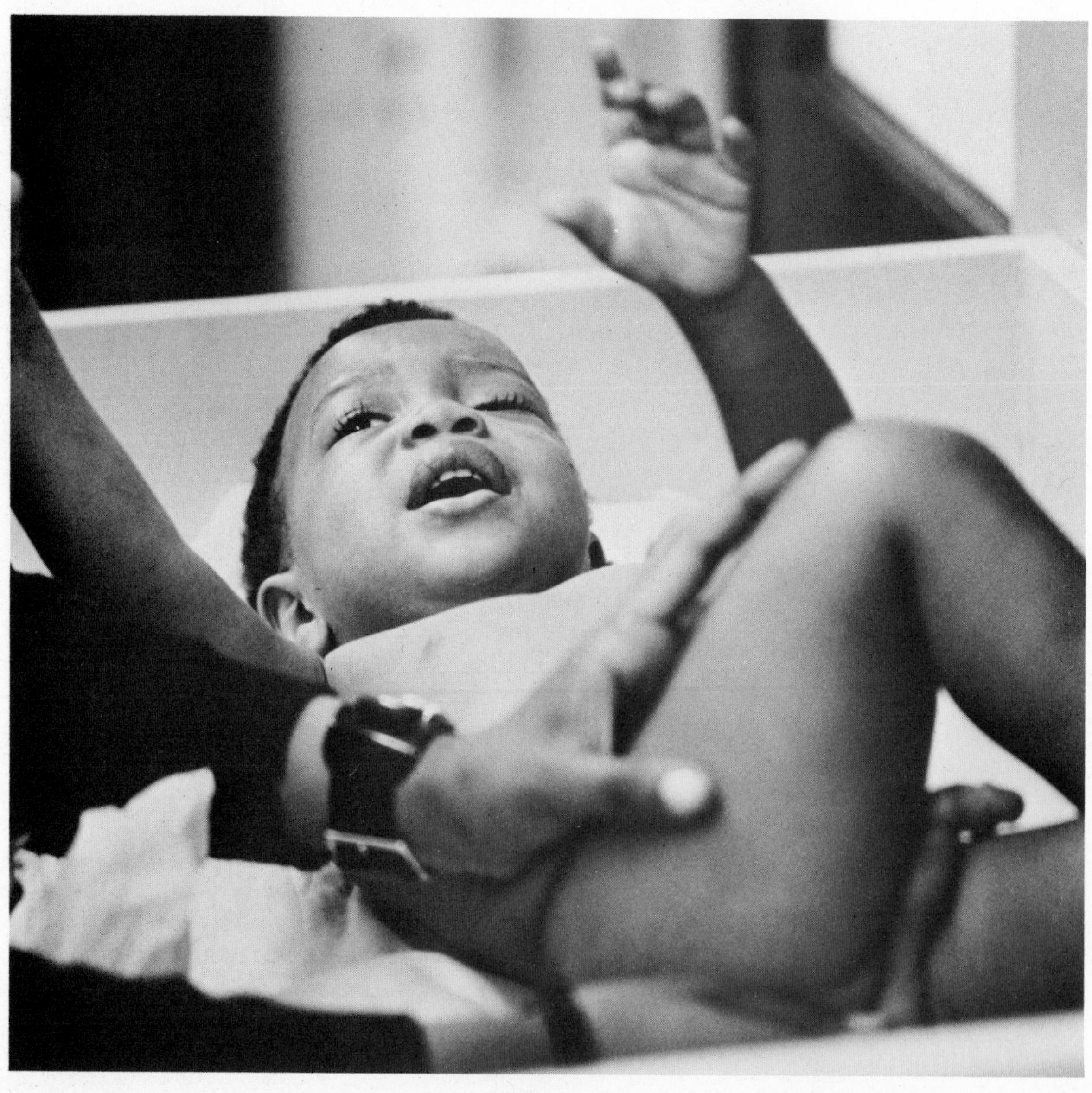

83

84

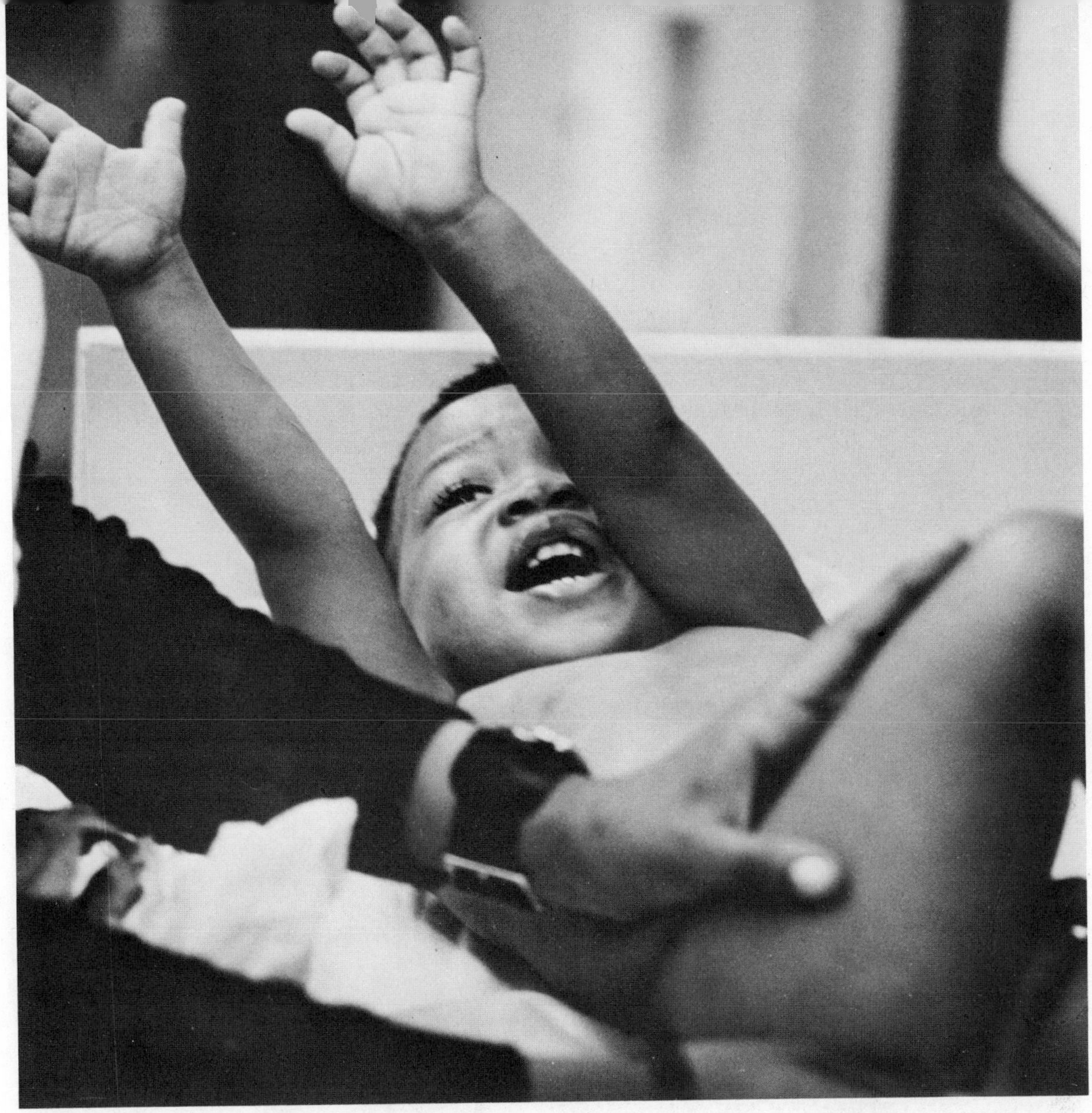

85

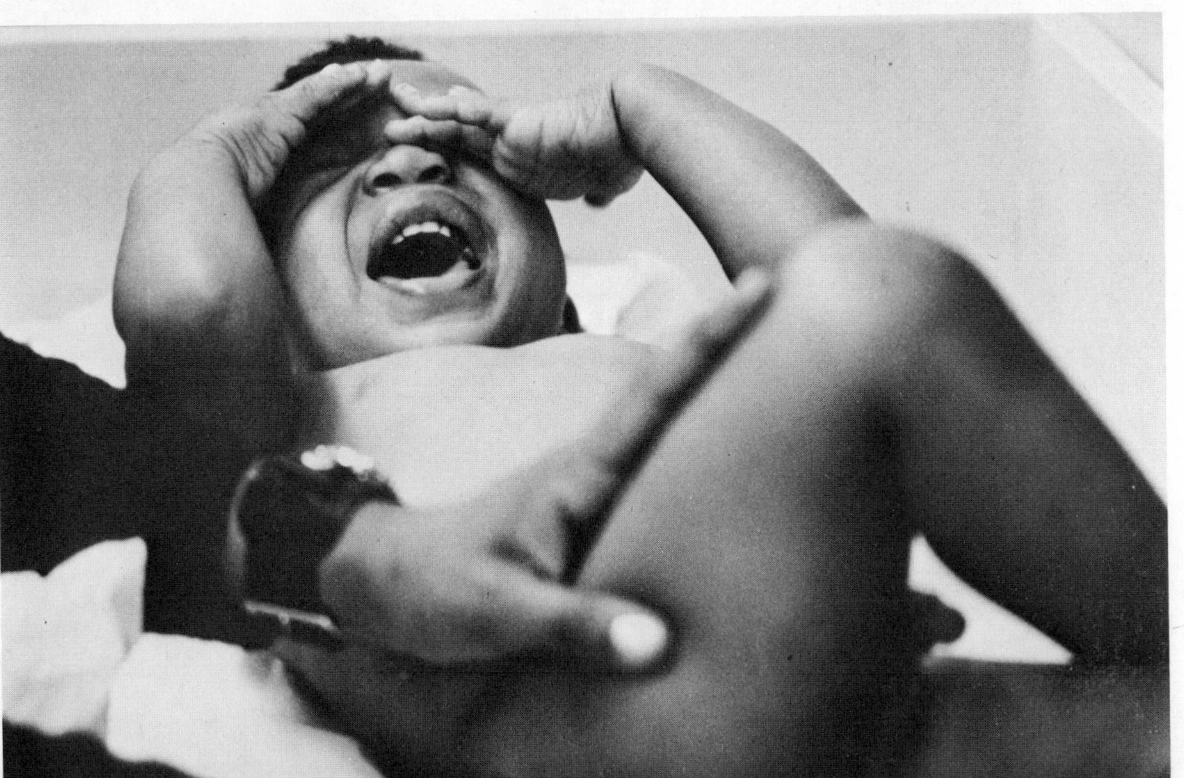

In contrast, we see in PHOTOGRAPHS 86, 87, and 88 a five-year-old girl who is being examined by the pediatrician. The two band-aids on her fingers bear witness that blood tests are being made. She has cooperated with the doctor at every step. On and on it goes. She is not stoic, she is resigned. *That's the way grownups do it. Open your mouth. Say "Ah," breathe deep, big, bigger, that's right. No, it doesn't hurt, but why are the grownups always poking at you? Bet they don't do it to the other grownups.*

This young child has been in and out of doctors' offices and clinics with a blood condition which is resistant to treatment. As recorded in the photographs, she is the model patient. It should not be concluded that the experience was delight throughout. If she looks rather subdued in PHOTOGRAPH 88, it is because, now through with all tests and ex-

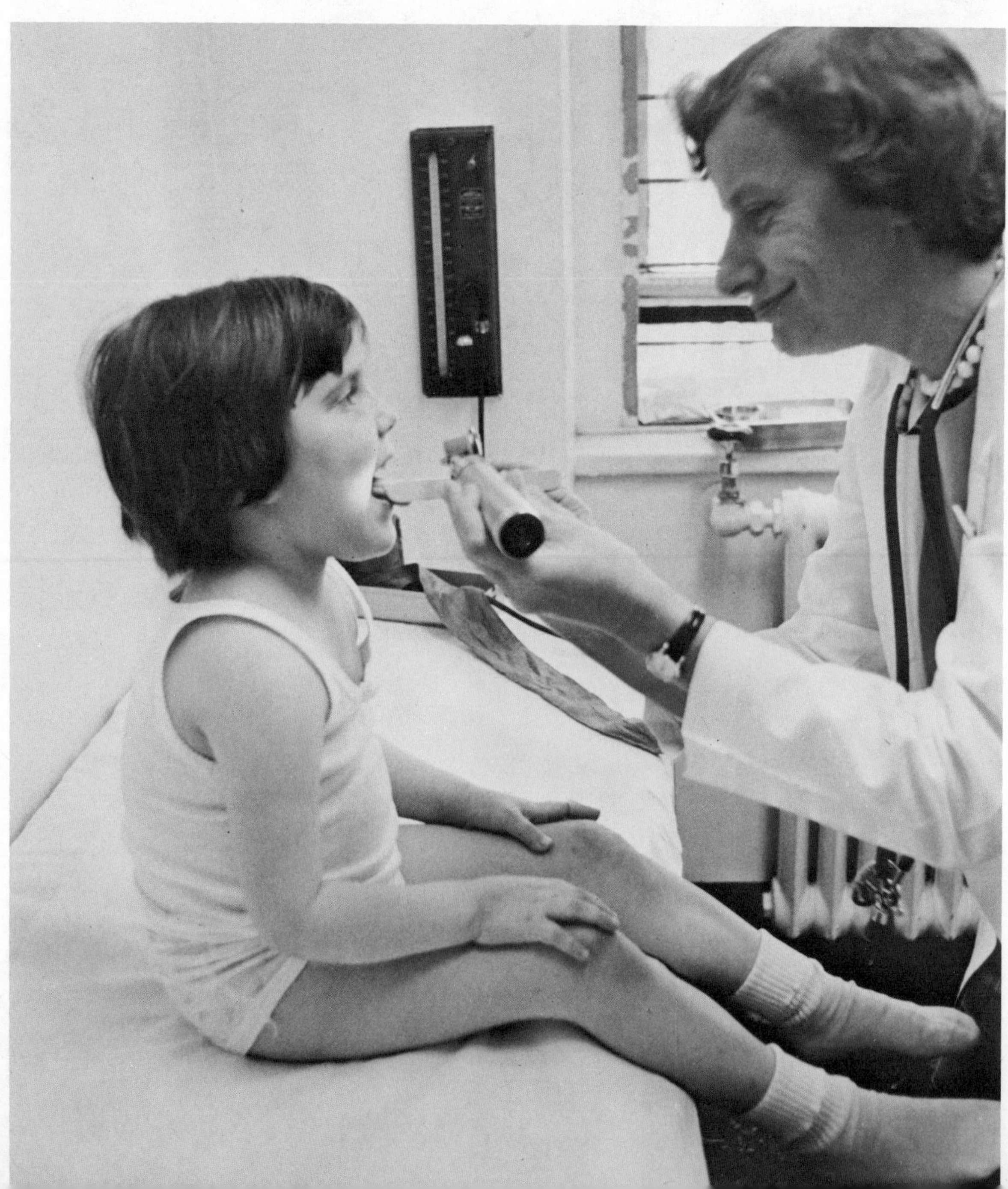

86

aminations, she wants to be told she may go home. It's time to ruminate. *Doctors and doctors, nurses and nurses. The needles and the shots. Why me? Suzy, Jamie, they don't have to go to the doctor's all the time. I didn't do nothing. Why do I get punished? The grownups say it's to keep healthy. I am healthy. I am like the others. I run as fast as Suzy. Maybe I'll get to be the champ, and then what are the grownups going to say?* A great deal of self-questioning and also controlled hostility, with the resentment just showing through her apparently placid expression.

In any large group of children, one is sure to find a few who disclaim reactions to painful stimuli. The next photographs show five children who are determined to make of their visit to the clinic a playful experience. They have had, or will have, to go through the routines of temperature-taking, finger-

87

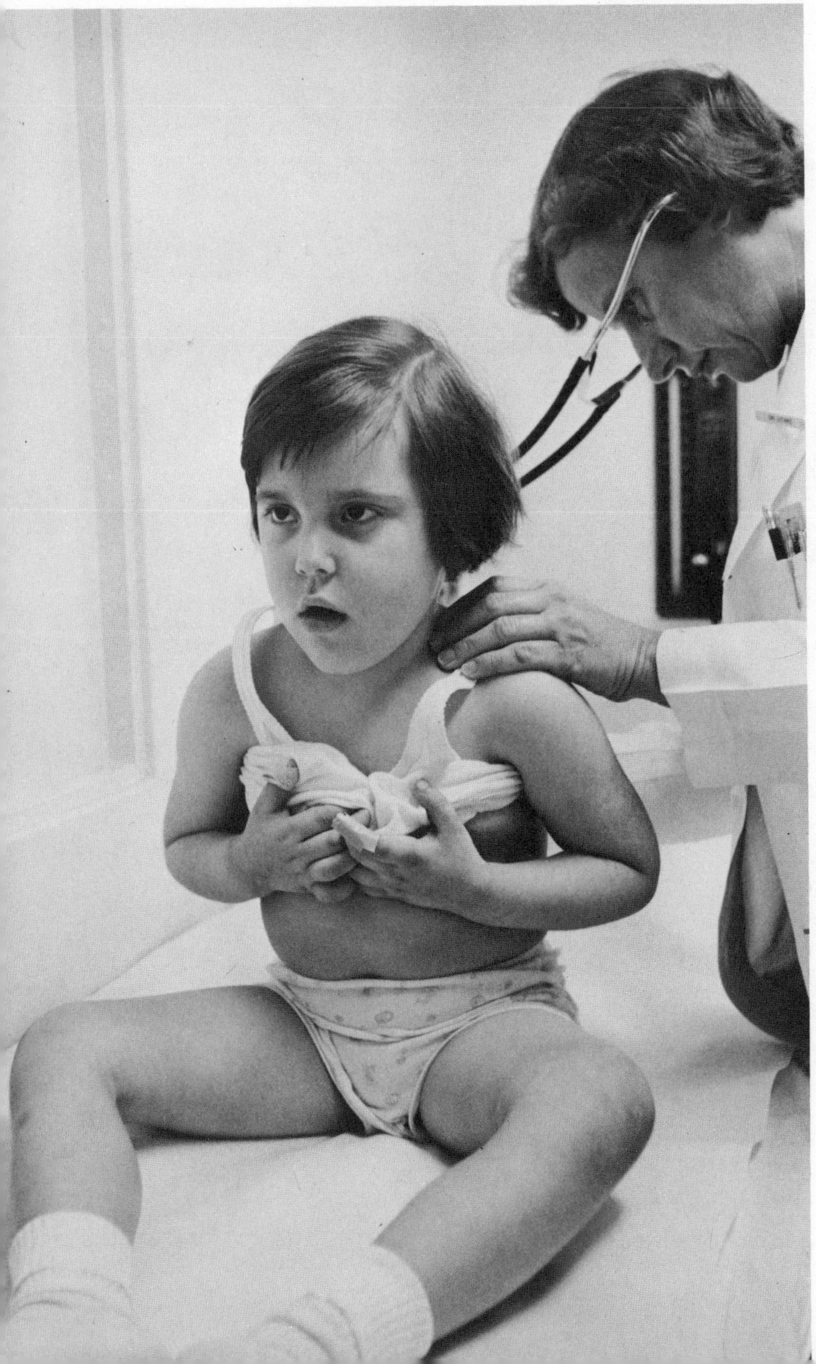

88

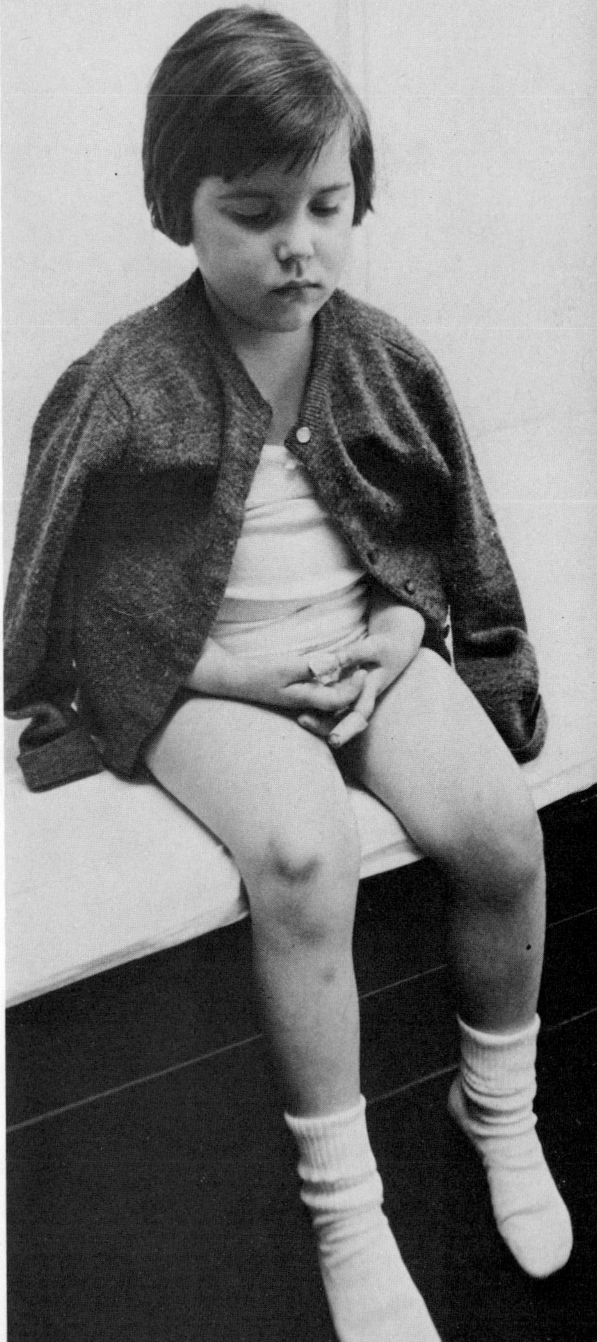

pricking, complete examination. Nothing is going to alter their merrymaking—*nothing until the accompanying adult without ceremony grabs your hand to take you home or to the pediatrician's office.*

In PHOTOGRAPHS 89 and 90, a three-year-old boy and a two-and-a-half-year-old girl seem mesmerized by the photographer's assistant who explains the presence of the camera and how they (the children) can go on as they please. This is just what these two children had intended to do anyhow. Adults and children in the background may well sit patiently, waiting for their turn, but these

89

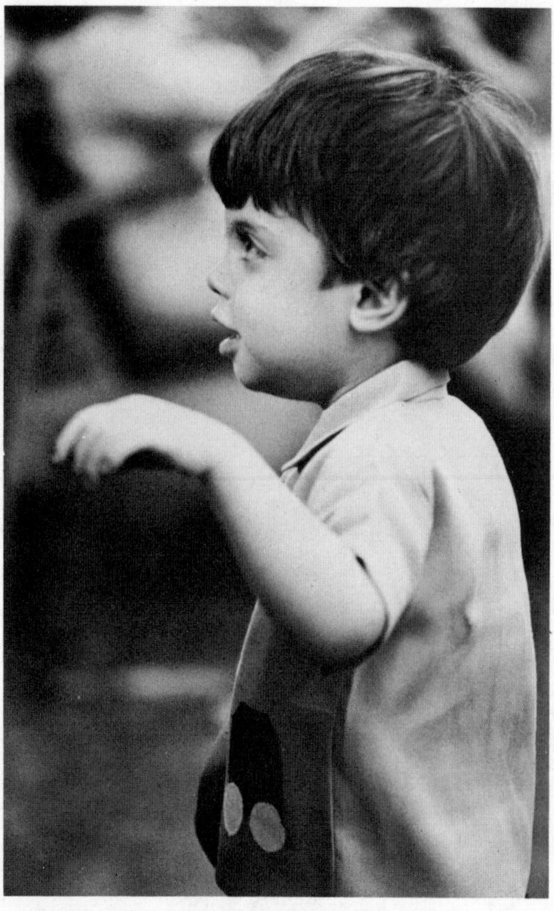

90

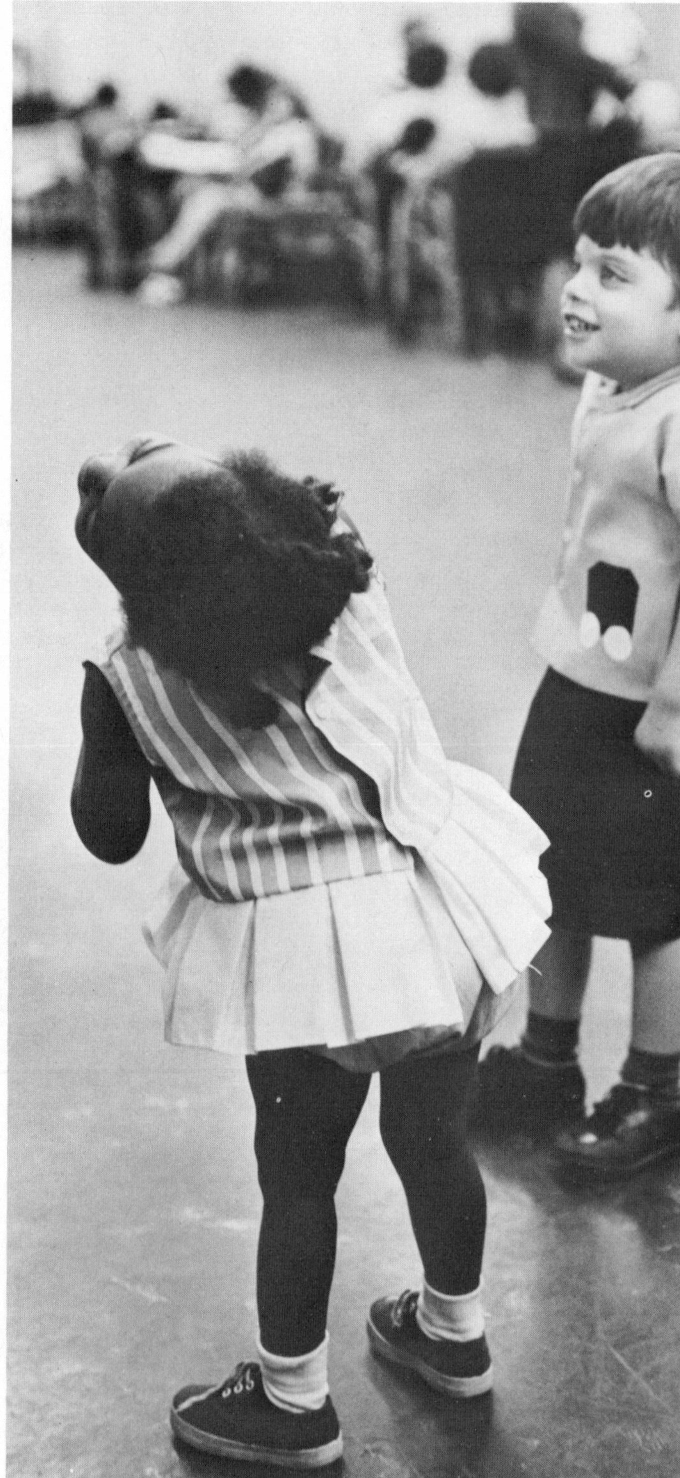

two (and a five-year-old boy who joins the fun in PHOTOGRAPH 91) have shaken off any serious purpose. The waiting room can be a racetrack or a baseball field. You just make it so. The three-year-old boy in particular is totally oblivious of what is to come. For him, even Those Shots have no sinister overtones. *Just laugh it off and you don't even know if it happened.* We see him in PHOTOGRAPH 91 building a plane, emulating the five-year-old boy who is racing through free space with his own already tested flying machine. *Well, will mine fly? That big boy made his plane neat and does it go full speed ahead!*

This is a serious enterprise. He would feel as big as that five-year-old if only this corner and that would flatten down and his plane became "neat"; then he would be just like the bigger boy. *He thinks he's so great. Wait till I get mine just like yours—then, what will you say?* In PHOTOGRAPH 92 he has given up. Forcibly hitched up onto a box by Mother to wait his turn for examination, he hangs on to the now shapeless paper that was to make him the worthy rival of "that big boy." If he must wait, he will, a little sobered up, but untroubled, making ready for the next laugh.

91

92

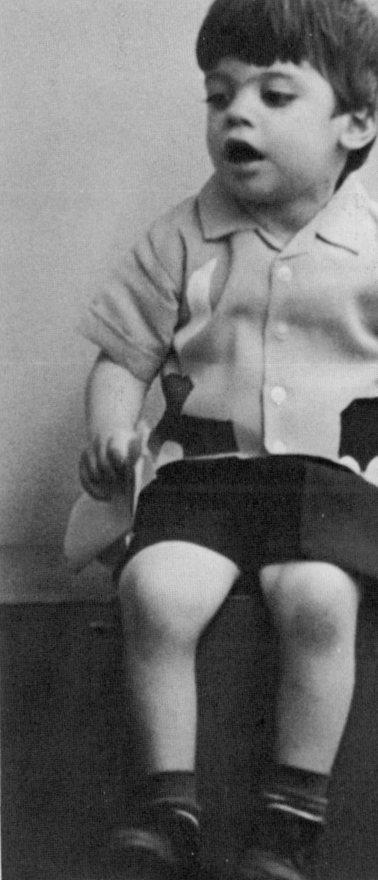

The four- and six-year-old boys in PHOTOGRAPH 93 are shadow-playing baseball, the younger one caught in the facsimile of a pitch, his general's hat tucked into his belt, while the older one is at the ready for that phantom ball. If they can't have the garb, they can at least have the stance. The action is so rapid and energetic that in PHOTOGRAPH 94 the six-year-old is about to shed his pants, his navel in full view. The general's hat has

93

94

been brushed aside to reveal a picture collected from a table, but he goes on pitching, while the five-year-old behind him, who had not dared join the game, is forcibly pulled away from the scene. No escape for him. A big hand is wrapped around his own. No resistance is possible. He was only a spectator; still he was enjoying the show. He knows he is being marshaled into the doctor's office, and the prospect is obviously not to his liking. He is controlling his anger, very well indeed for his age. If the inner voice were to break through, Mom would not like the sound of it. *Just when you're beginning to have fun, it's those needles again. Don't talk and be still and do what the doctor tells you to do. Like fun it is for my own good. Maybe another mother—No, you can't change your mother—keep the one you got—Johnny has no mother, and Smitty has two mothers. But I wanted to stay here, and there I go, pulled by the hand like a baby.*

The attitude of this little boy is quite in contrast to the carefree and "devil may care" conduct of the jolly ones we have seen. Their turn will come, but they don't feel they have to wait for that moment in fear of pain. When it comes, it comes, and that's that. Meanwhile *—well now, what can we do? A race! With rubber soles, they'll let you gallop on hard floors. So, let's go!*

17

Parent-child associates

Children are what the mothers are.
No fondest father's fondest care
Can fashion so the infant heart.
WALTER SAVAGE LANDOR, *Children*

We are familiar with the mother-child motif in art and literature. However, we note that even the beautiful paintings of the Renaissance show little concern for the inner life of their subjects. Our modest preoccupation is at the opposite pole: we aim to project feelings and thoughts, as they can be caught without posing, without warning or preparation.

In PHOTOGRAPHS 95, 96, and 97, we follow a dramatic sequence of communication, and lack of it. In PHOTOGRAPH 95, the mother, probably preoccupied with the outcome of the pediatrician's examination, has momentarily lost contact with her fourteen-month-old baby girl; at least this is what the baby perceives. Body contact is there, the child pressing on her mother's body and the mother's hands lying on the little one's shoulders. Yet, it is clear that communication has been interrupted. Those big eyes are full of anxiety. They seem to implore the return of something that is now missing, and plead for an explanation. *Perhaps Mother does not love me any more. What is she thinking of? Not about me. Who is going to love me like Mommy does?* These are fleeting, but intense, reactions. Words are not available yet, but they are not necessary for expression. In the following picture, PHOTOGRAPH 96, the mother has "returned" and the child's face reflects the newly

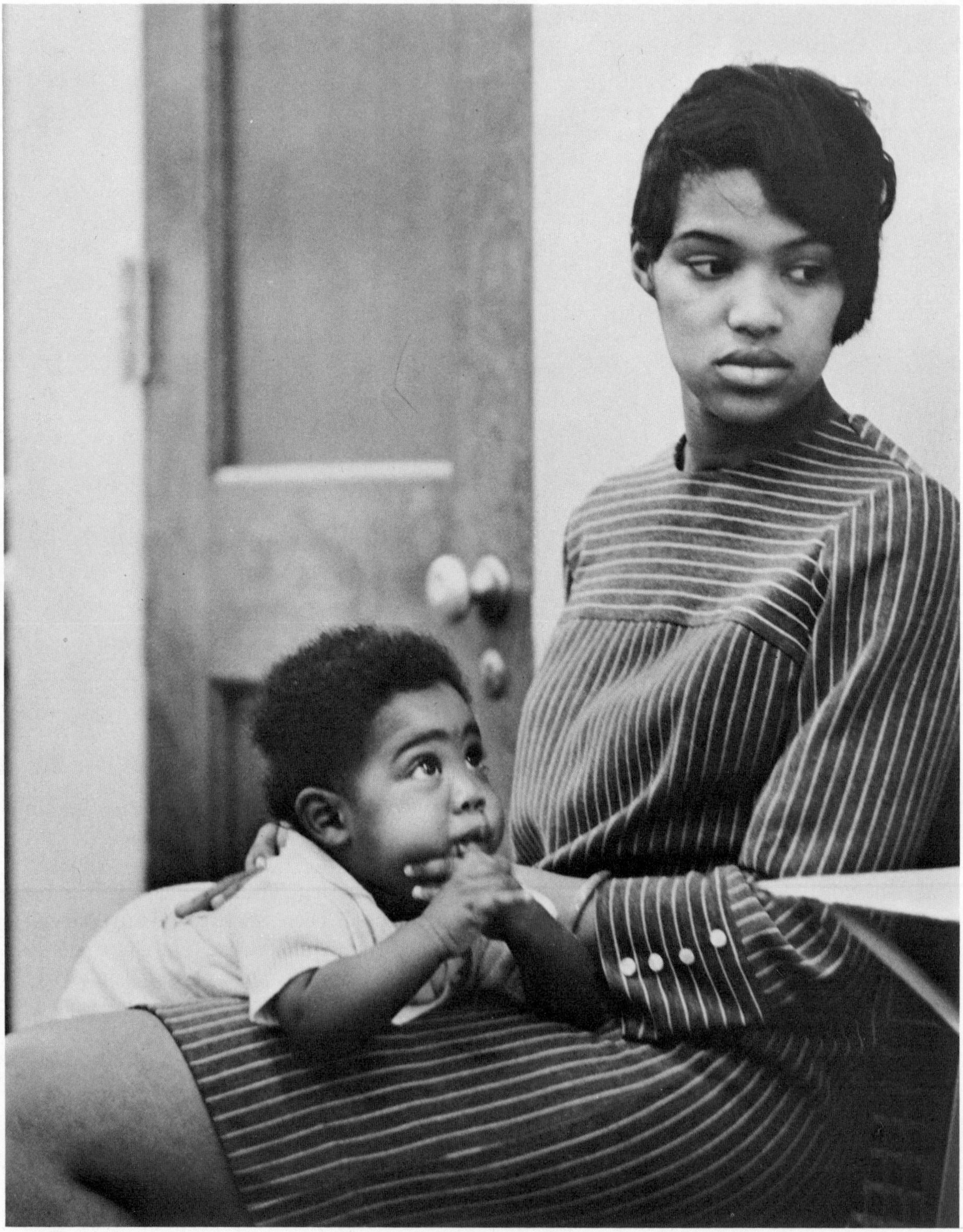

97

restored security. Her anguish has visibly lessened and, in PHOTOGRAPH 97, she has fully recovered. Curious about the unfamiliar environment, she is free to look about without the tenacious worry that *perhaps Mother—*. Throughout this sequence she has been sucking her fingers for physical (she is teething) and emotional comfort—a familiar behavior pattern.

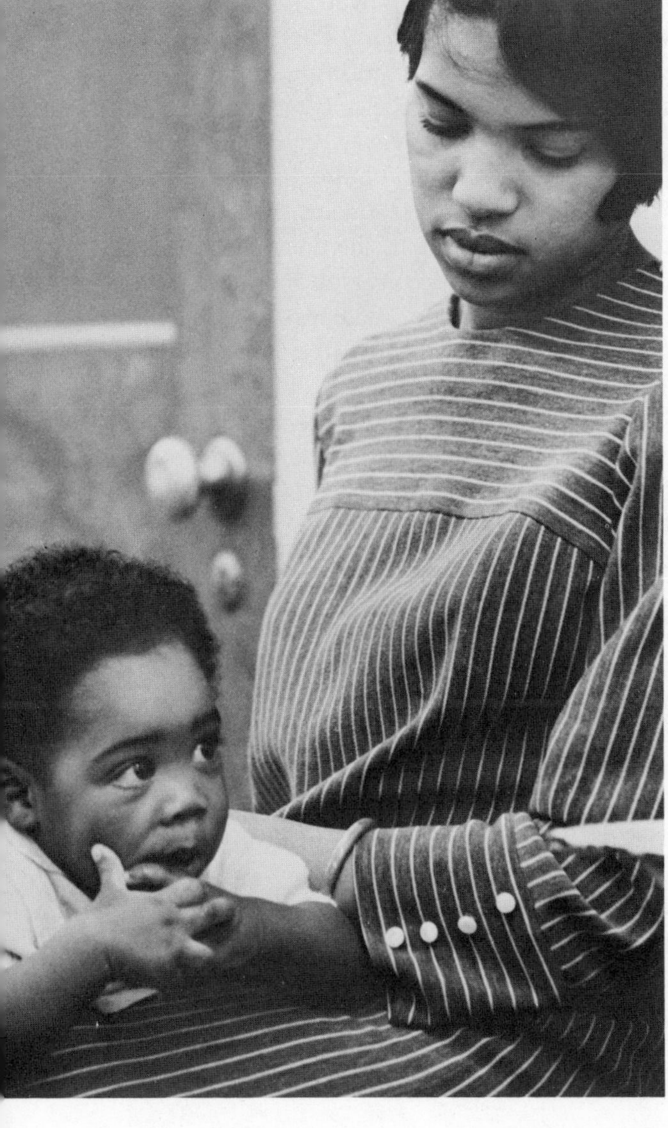

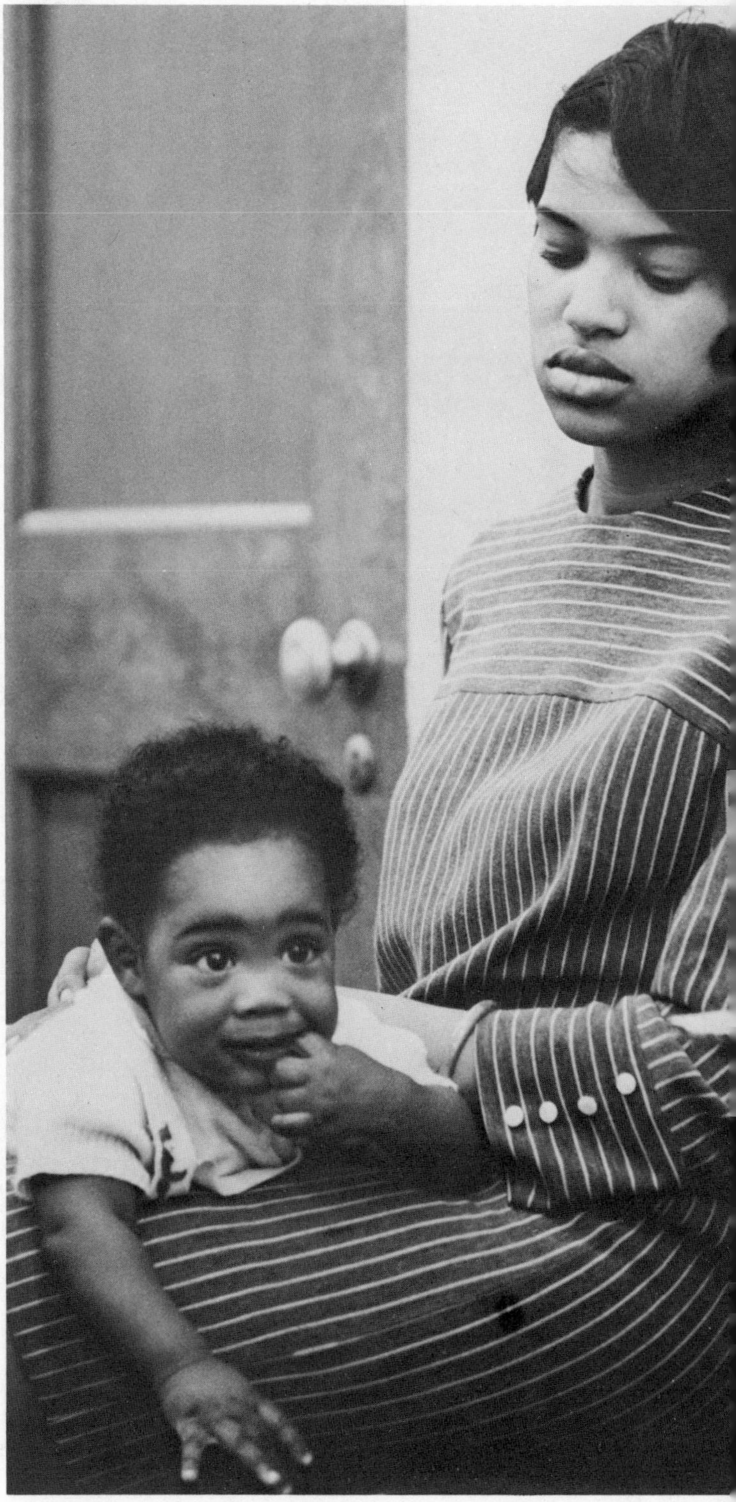

98

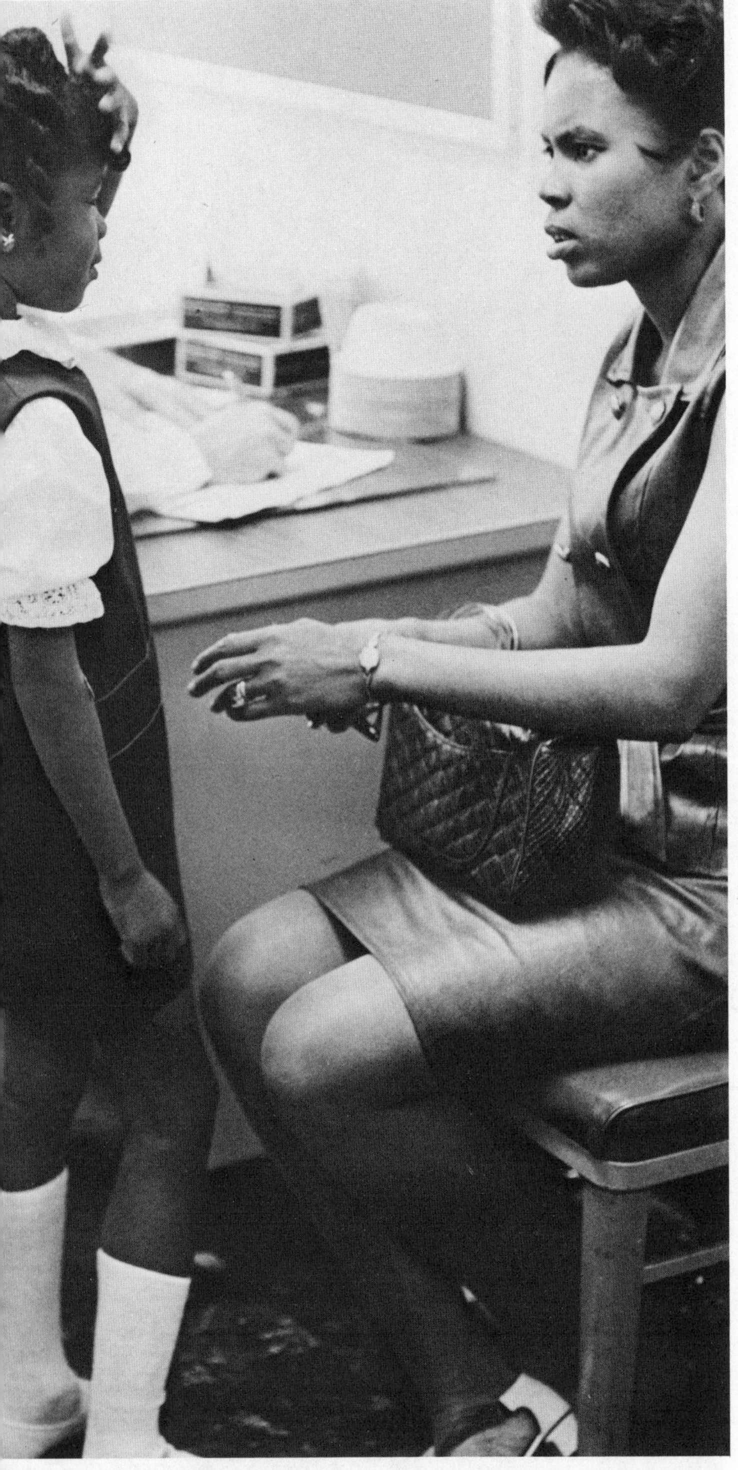

PHOTOGRAPH 98 illustrates a moment of child-parent communication, whereas the previous group threw light on a parent-child communication. The eight-year-old girl has been examined by the pediatrician, who is now writing her report. Incidentally, children are seldom specific about the location of their symptoms (some adults can also be vague, even as they firmly expect an accurate diagnosis). The child now thinks of one more complaint. For good measure perhaps. The "pointing" hand is deployed above the forehead and part of the hair. The facial expression is not one of great suffering; in fact, there is lingering a near smile not very relevant to the suddenly discovered symptom. The mother, however, has immediately reacted with alarm and puzzlement. She wonders whether she should call the doctor's attention to this new indication, which might make an important difference in her evaluation. A wealth of descriptive detail follows, which somehow, in time, reassures the mother. *It hurts here, no, it hurts there—it just began, no, I remember it started yesterday—it's like it pounds, no it scratches—I fell on my head when I was playing stickball, maybe that's why it hurts.*

In general, and almost without exception, children are ambivalent toward illness. (Aren't adults themselves hanging on to this prerogative?) On the one hand, there are the pain or the discomfort, the restriction of activities, the ingestion of nasty-tasting medicines and tasteless, detested foods, the separation from one's friends. But there is also a world of compensation: the helplessness which makes Mother indispensable, full of love and attention as if one were a baby again. Like our eight-year-old girl at the clinic, even though she is not sick in the sense here referred to, children unconsciously capitalize on their symptoms. This is a common regression—a regression which can in some cases go as far as complete helplessness and dependence on maternal love and care (regression to the womb).

In PHOTOGRAPH 99 we see again the sixteen-month-old boy who vociferously protested the temperature-taking in Chapter 15. Completely relaxed now, his fingers still in his mouth for additional pleasure, he has forgotten the tough endurance test, he has forgiven Mother for her part in it! All of this is reflected in the mother's face. Here is her loving baby again, and she is obviously happy that her relationship with the child has returned to normal.

99

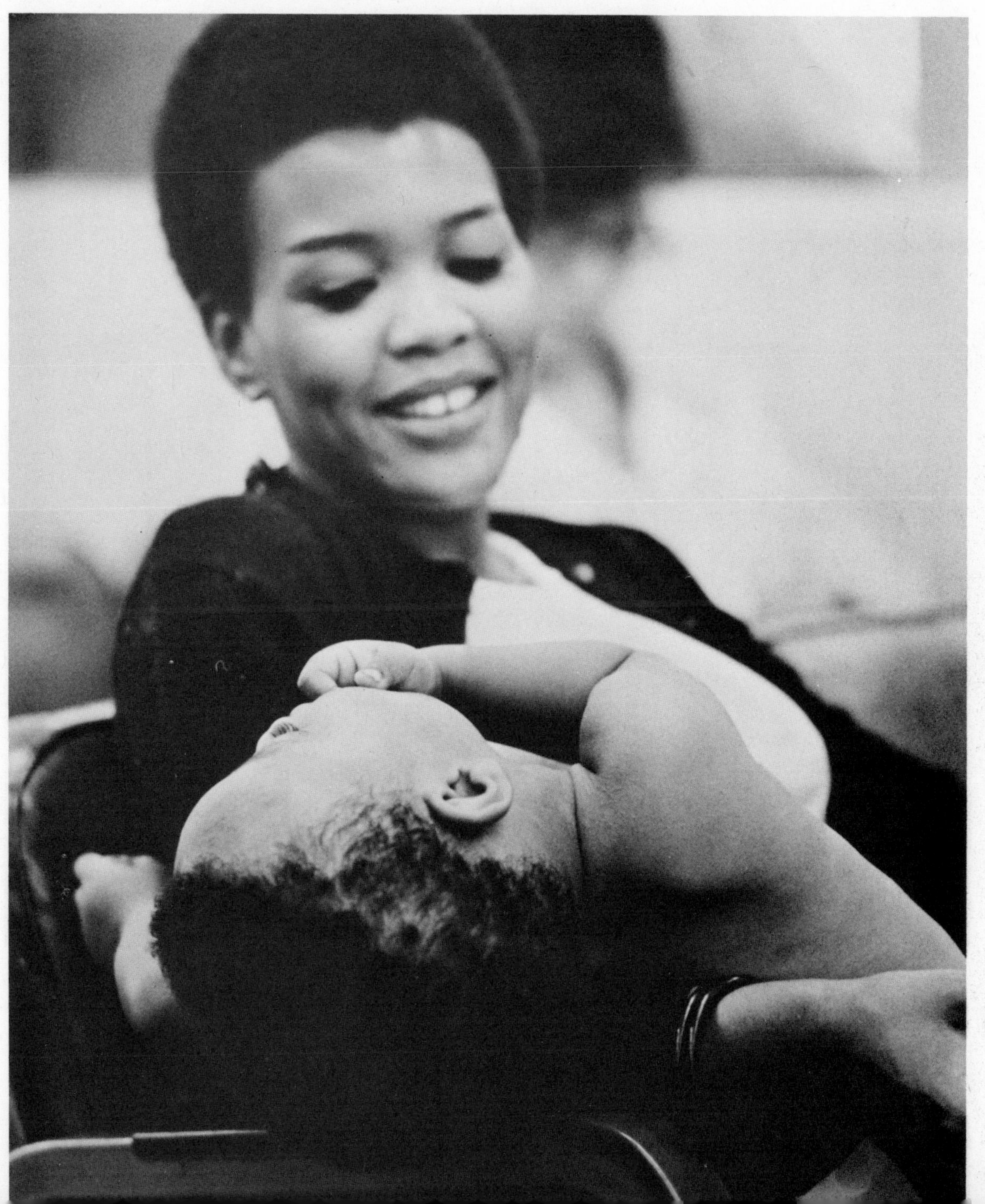

PHOTOGRAPH 100 projects a father-son communication, along with an identification that is not only physical, even if it appears predominantly that. The boy is eight years old and, ever since he was able to walk and talk, he has announced to his world that "just like Daddy" is his way of life. Despite the accumulated studies of child-parent identification, there is no fast rule regarding its beginnings and its evolution. Very young children call any man "Daddy"—their father, or other men familiar to their home. If a boy has no father, he must fantasy one. A five-year-old boy, whose father deserted his mother when he was only a few months old, came for treatment because of his extremely aggressive and

100

destructive behavior toward people, of all ages, and inanimate objects (furniture, personal belongings) as well. The mother had not remarried, but male companionship was not wanting; any man who came close enough to this boy was immediately claimed by him as a father. Embarrassing occasionally. His play was revealing; it revolved mostly around a father-son relationship, with a strict but loving father named after the current male friend of his mother. The fantasy was not without frustration, as the current father figure would vanish. He came in fact to feel that a male figure was vulnerable, and expressed his fear that he would not and could not become a man. This is an extreme case, one, however, that shows dramatically the need of the young boy for identification with his father, or a male figure in the absence of the father.

To get back to our eight-year-old boy and his father, it was a red-letter day when the ophthalmologist indicated that he, too, must wear glasses. "Like Daddy" again. You could not sell him the idea of trying to lose weight, even if football is looming rather large in his future. No, like Daddy. Communication between father and son here is easy and productive, tending to be a little exclusive of any and all about them.

18

Even work can be fun

> Now the colored pencils in action. The green one, by a mere whirl of the wrist, could be made to produce a ruffled tree, or the eddy left by a submerged crocodile. The blue one drew a simple line across the page—and the horizon of all seas was there . . . The white one alone, that lanky albino among pencils, kept its original length, or at least did so until I discovered that, far from being a fraud leaving no mark on the page, it was the ideal implement since I could imagine whatever I wished while I scrawled.
>
> VLADIMIR NABOKOV, *Speak, Memory*

The photographs in this chapter were taken at the Goddard Riverside Community School. They are principally concerned with artistic and shop work done by children in the age group of eight to twelve. In PHOTOGRAPH 101, we see a boy who is starting a portrait. He has announced that it is going to be a girl, but as is the case with not-too-experienced artists, it ends up being somewhat of a self-portrait, the mop of hair and the bangs prominent, then trailing into a facial outline reminiscent of the hippie sartorial style. It's not easy to do a painting job with background to bring out your subject's personality and mix and arrange the colors the way the experts must do it.

The facial contortions in PHOTOGRAPH 102 may not add to the artistic value, but the tension, the will to do it are there, and best results are expected. Let anyone make fun of his work of art and you'll hear our budding artist take care of the critic. Not a Leonardo da Vinci, not a Rembrandt, but he is very satisfied with his work. The facial contractions over, he basks in unabashed pride. He's done it; even if the background has now overwhelmed the portrait, he has painted the "girl" as he wanted to.

101

102

PHOTOGRAPH 103 has caught a nine-year-old boy who is ready to leave for home with his treasure. He has needed help for measurements and drafting, but at this point let it be known that the shelves he has put together are unquestionably his property. The teacher who stands by has no intention of claiming any property rights—it is understood that the shelves can be taken home—but look at that right hand and the determined, almost belligerent, facial expression. The hand moves so fast, it is out of focus, and the face says clearly: *This is mine, I made it, and I take it home, nobody can stop me. My toys and my books are going to look great on the shelves. I worked hard on them, and they'll fit perfect in my room.* The teacher has understood, he simply observes the underground explosion with an amused smile. He knows that each child has an unlimited sense of ownership and pride in the objects he or she has created, however slight the achievement may be. Children feel so small, so weak in comparison with adults that they must attempt to compensate with grandiose fantasies. You may think that what you are seeing here is five boards nailed in a certain configuration. Certainly not; it is perceived as a masterpiece of cabinetmaking. Neither father nor big brother would do it any better!

103

104

In PHOTOGRAPHS 104 and 105 we see Alice, eight years old, who is pondering over what she might do in the art room before actually going in. Woodwork, clay, painting, drawing, all the materials are available. No problem here, *but what to do? The boys always know what they want and they go ahead and DO it. The tables are inviting, just reach out for the paint pots (look at him, he knows what colors he wants); maybe clay, I could make a small pot, an ashtray, but it always ends up a funny shape.* Still on her guard, she advances imperceptibly, hands over her mouth in an almost supplicatory attitude. *The boys are going to make fun of me; well, maybe they're too busy to notice me. I'll try a little dish for Mom's bobbypins, that's not too hard and the teacher will help me, she does the thing for me. Let's see what they're doing?*

105

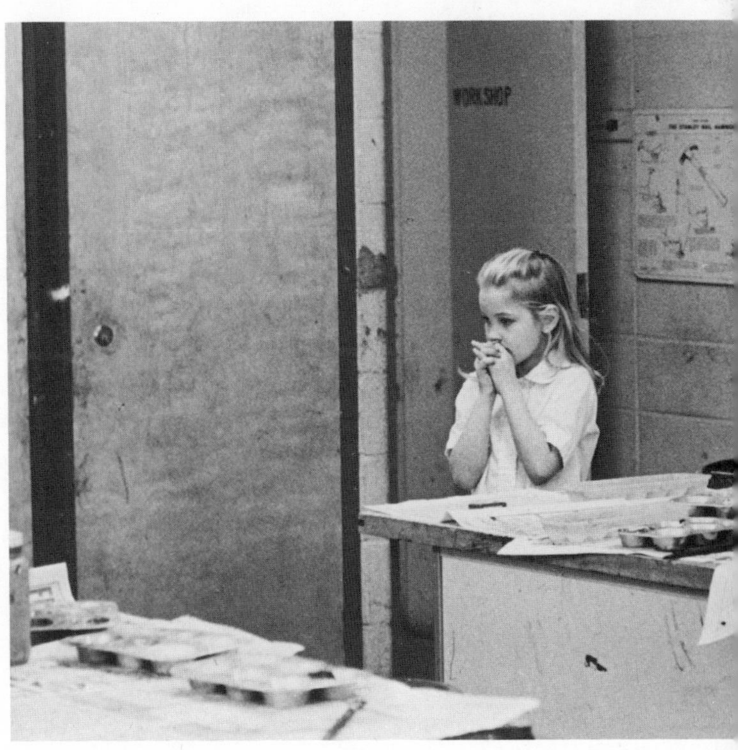

Oh, this one (PHOTOGRAPH 106), *he's really doing scribble scrabble except it's with a brush, and it looks like something, a design I think. Just the same, it's pretty hard. Two colors already. I wish I could paint like that.*

Alice does not seem to get great satisfaction out of watching the boy, even if she dares to think that with some lines here, some lines there, she too could make a picture. No, the boys are better. Still, she approaches the table; the boy, totally unaware of her presence, fills in spaces around his design with a uniform coating to provide a background. She follows every stroke of the

106

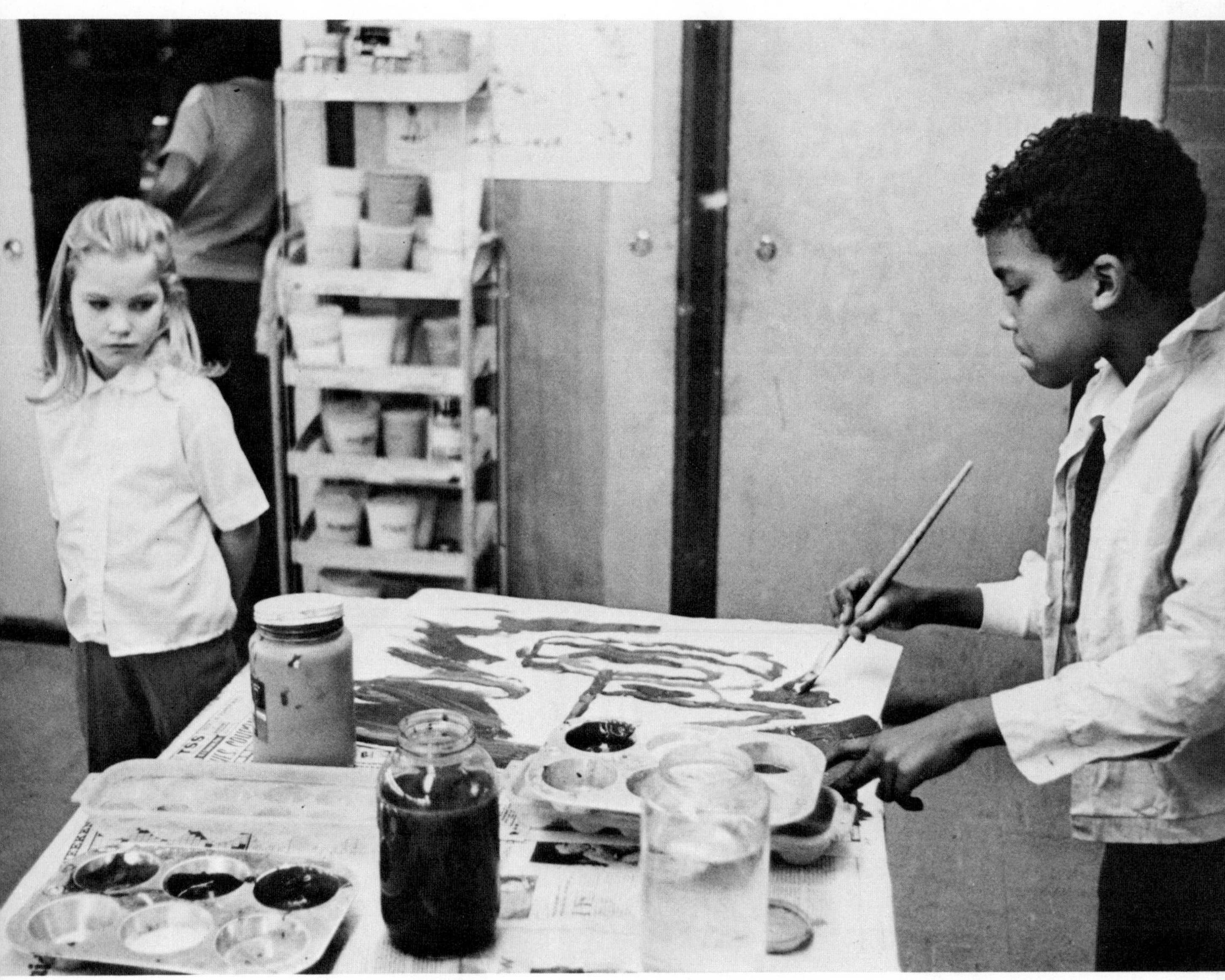

brush with an attentive but somewhat dejected expression. In the meantime, that other boy starts a new picture (PHOTOGRAPH 107). *Those boys are so sure of themselves.* It turns out to be a duplicate of his first picture. *So what? He can paint. But me? When they're grown up, they'll probably get those millions for their stuff like those great painters they told us about on TV. Funny, they're always men, those big shots.*

And so we leave Alice to her ruminating voices before she settles down to modeling her little "chickens" and eggs, all about the same format.

107

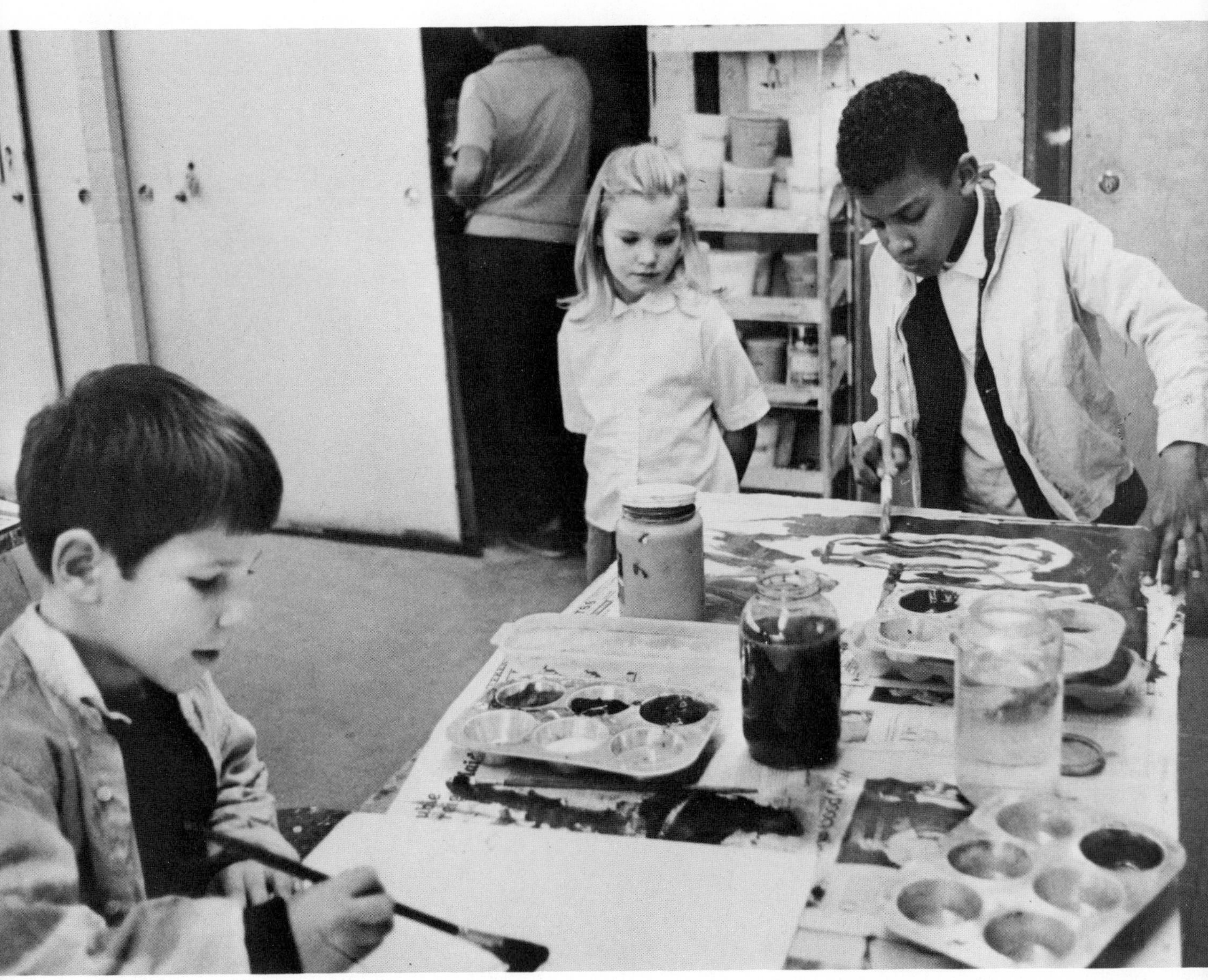

19

Where does the first step lead?

> Adam was but human—this explains it all. He did not want the apple for the apple's sake, he wanted it only because it was forbidden.
>
> MARK TWAIN, *Pudd'nhead Wilson*

Teen-age smoking has always been a source of concern to parents—especially those who, themselves addicted to smoking, have a strong sense of guilt regarding it and attempt to "save their children from a nasty habit." The first cigarette is attempted earlier and earlier, and the ten-to-twelve age group is now involved. The attitudes of individuals and organizations toward smoking are confusing to children. "A cigarette can kill you"/"Every puff brings you. . . ."—now, which? More vulnerable than adults, teen-agers alternate between wild enthusiasm for the smoke on the one hand, and guilt and depression over the anticipated cancer on the other.

In these photographs we have an unusual record of a first experience with smoking. Margie, thirteen, and Janet, fourteen, have long been friends. Janet, however, has a small edge on Margie: having become acquainted with cigarettes, she takes pleasure in educating her peers to a new pastime. Although the girls know that the photographer is around, they are not acutely aware of his presence, and the images are spontaneous.

In PHOTOGRAPH 108, Janet, the dark-haired girl, quite at ease, cigarette in hand, is inviting Margie to share the fun with her. Margie is somewhat shocked, and very reluctant to accept the invitation. *What will my mother*

108

say if she finds out? The subject was never brought up so maybe it wouldn't be so terrible if she knew. Still, she doesn't approve of smoking—cancer and all that jazz. But maybe one cigarette wouldn't hurt. Janet does it, she doesn't look like she was going to have cancer. Well, try and see. It will take a little getting used to it. What if I get sick? Janet is sure to make fun of me and tell all the kids I'm a square. There goes! O.K., I'll try one.

In PHOTOGRAPH 109, the fun is for Janet, who guffaws at Margie's awkwardness and naivete in even the simple gesture of lighting

110

the match. PHOTOGRAPH 110 concentrates on Margie's reaction to her first secret, possibly "forbidden," cigarette. A great disappointment. *Certainly not what the kids said it would be, a strange taste, the mouth feeling "funny." Maybe Mother is right about the cancer. Can't give up now though.* And so, on with the cigarette, but with little participation on Margie's part—the cigarette burns by itself and it is obvious that smoking will not be an additional adolescent pleasure for her. Furthermore, in PHOTOGRAPH 111, Margie is puzzled by Janet's mastery of the art, and delirious enjoyment of it. *Maybe she's making fun of me. But how could I catch up to her with one cigarette? Man! she must have smoked packs and packs. And look at that cigarette in the corner of her mouth! That sure is experience! Really hopeless, when you think of it.*

And when Janet tops her performance with a demonstration of ring blowing, in PHOTOGRAPH 112, it is almost too much for Margie. To the reader, the technique may not seem so expert (the rings put in only a ghostlike appearance before vanishing), but Margie is much impressed by the sophistication evidenced in the weak cloud of smoke. Were it not for her conviction that she could never attain such spectacular results, she might be tempted to continue experimenting. She must acknowledge that, even if her cigarette seems to have been smoked, it is not owing to any direct action of her own. Along with her discouragement, the guilt reaction (with a touch of disgust) is clearly legible in Margie's first—so far unsuccessful—attempt at smoking enjoyment. No, Janet has not made a convert.

111

112

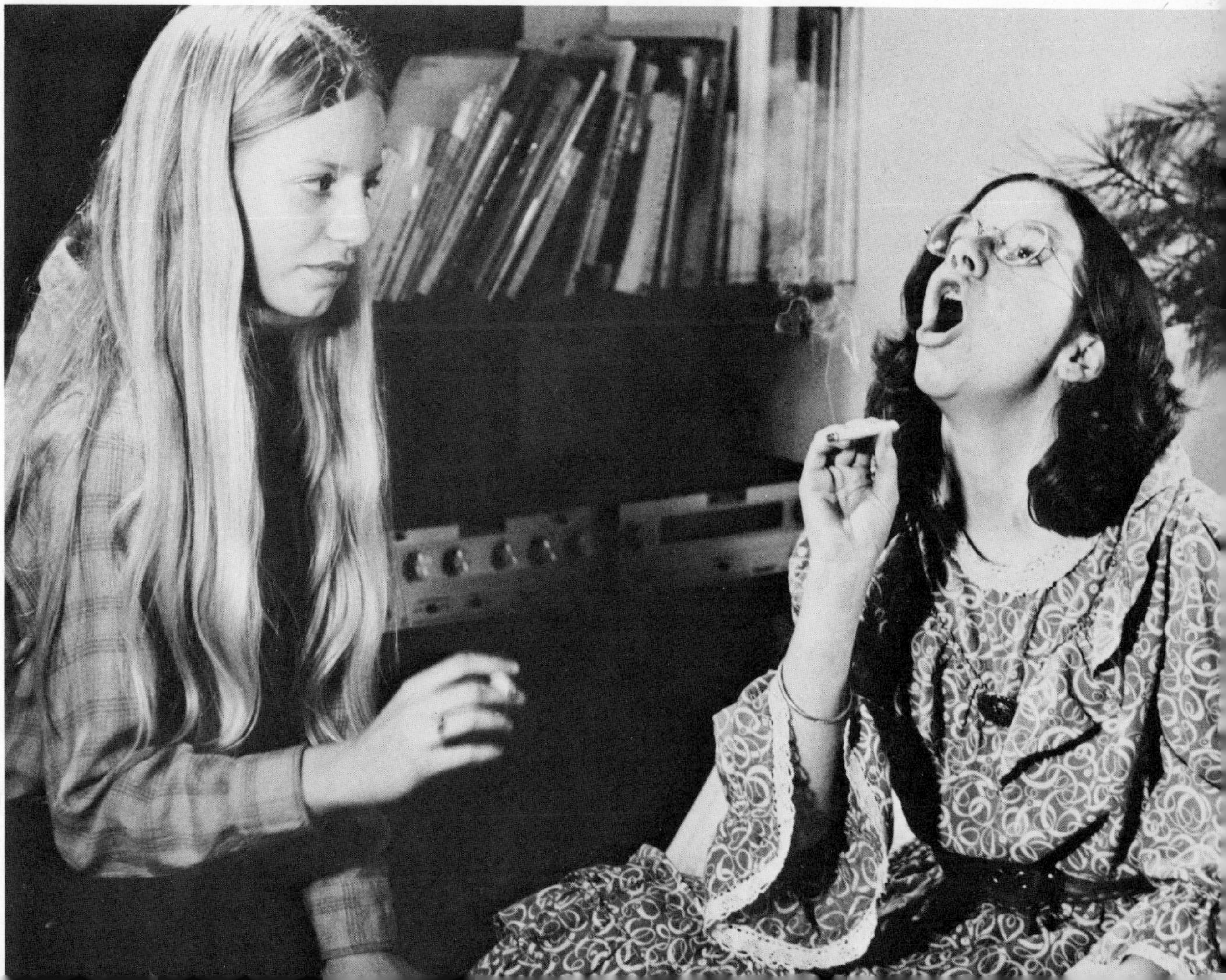

20

"Lost and found"

All losses are restored and sorrows end.
WILLIAM SHAKESPEARE, *Sonnet 30*

The photographs in this chapter were taken in the home of seven-year-old Karen. Our photographer spent considerable time getting acquainted with her and her mother, then becoming so unobtrusive that he could finally pass unnoticed—a candid photographer's trick, avoiding the "posed" look.

In PHOTOGRAPH 113, Karen is confiding "a secret" to her mother. This photograph is in contrast with the following two, where Karen reveals her "secret" in a playful mood. Indeed, this short sequence of images brings out, once more, the ambivalence so characteristic of the child's emotional life: having discovered that an upper incisor is loose, and though the experience is not new, she is at first reluctant to make a public announcement. Then, suddenly, her mouth is wide open as can be (PHOTOGRAPH 114), and she points with not too much precision to a space between two teeth. "Which one?" asks her mother. In PHOTOGRAPH 115, the tooth is precisely located. In these two pictures there is a kind of bravado, mixed with the elation that accompanies a happy event. Anticipation of the prize or reward she is bound to get for that soon-to-be-missing tooth may contribute to her cheerfulness.

The fundamental ambivalence is there, nevertheless, with or without reward. The

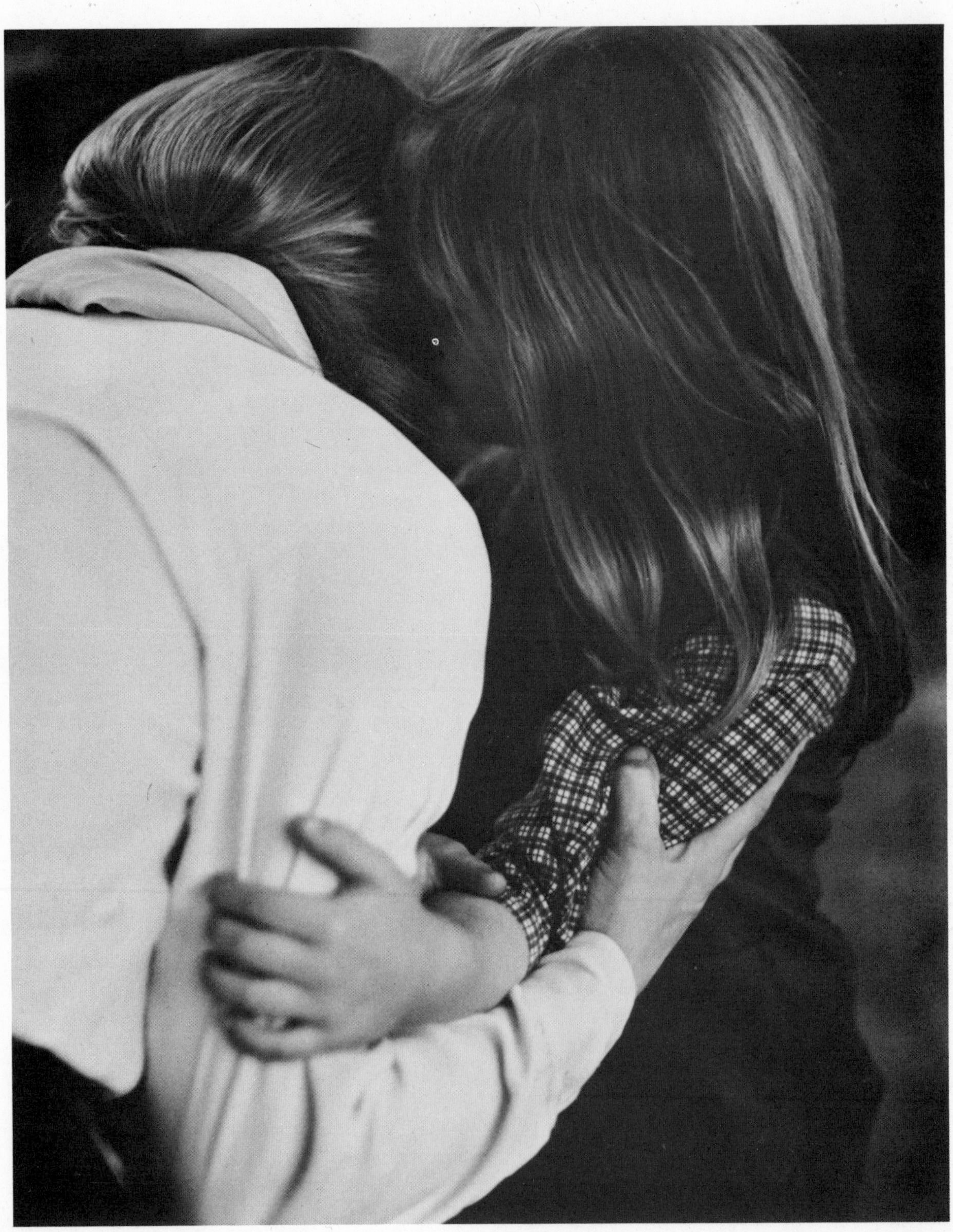

113

components of her emotional reaction are, on the one hand, the anxiety attached to any insult, however slight, to the body integrity, and, on the other hand, the pleasure of knowing that it will soon be over, that then she will be like all the other children whose mouths are variously shot with holes.

There is no denying that the reward plays a part, however. An eight-year-old girl, whose upper incisors were missing, came to my office for the first time. A casual comment on the vacancy was in order. It brought the cryptic reply, "In Boston I get a quarter and in New York I get a dollar." The parents were divorced and the child spent approximately equal periods of time in Boston, where the mother currently lived, and New York, which was the father's residence. The symbolic meaning of the money was clear, especially in the light of her experience with the parents: the mother, an alcoholic, was felt as the rejecting parent, while the father, though heavily burdened with business responsibilities, managed to get involved with the little girl within the limited time he could devote to her. These differences she had perceived. Little Karen has no split-reward problem; whatever her parents offer her as compensation for the loss will be accepted and turned into goodies of her choice.

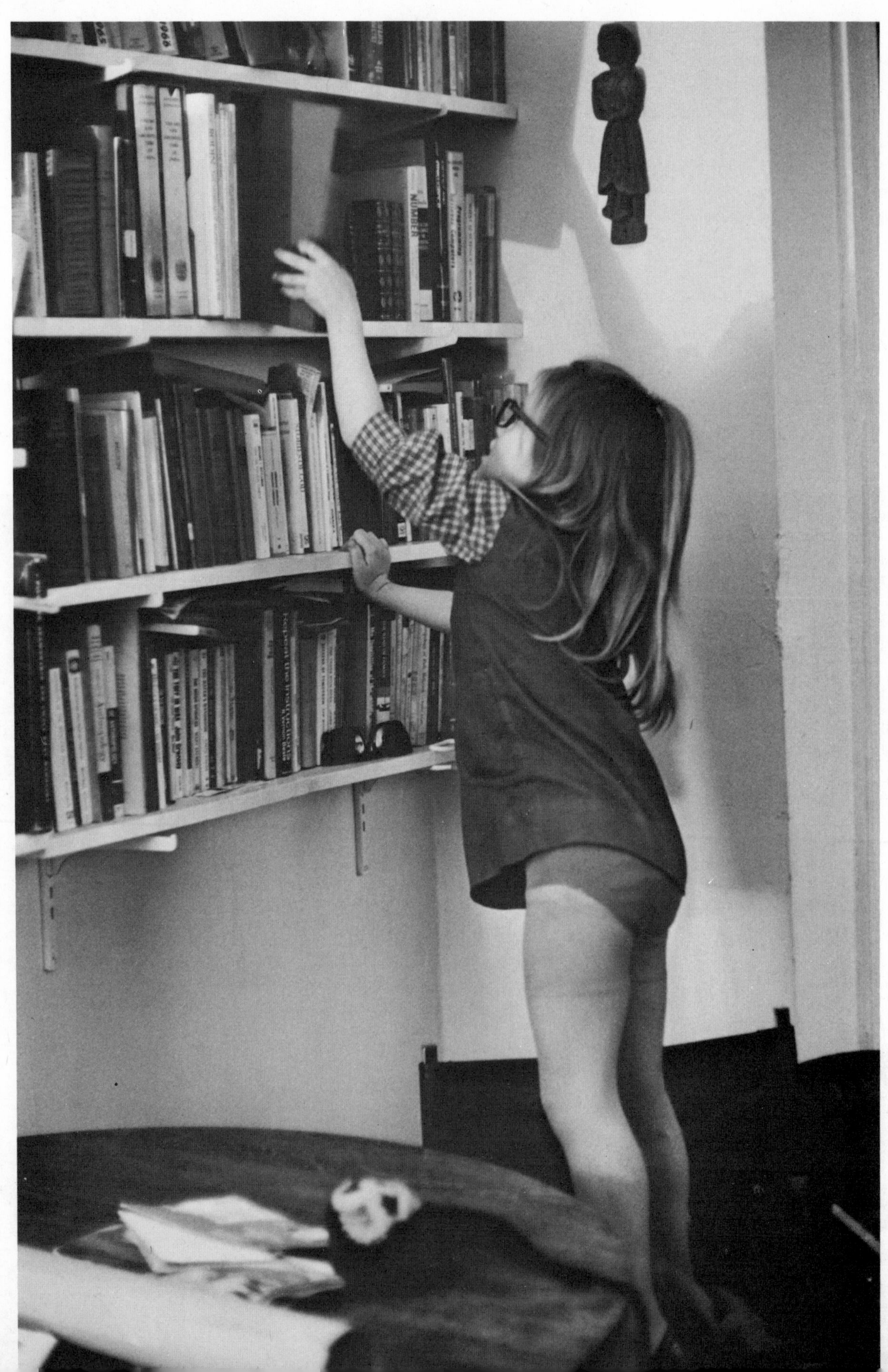

116

Karen's parents are literate people; the books displayed in their library reveal wide interests at a high level of culture. We see Karen in PHOTOGRAPH 116 climbing on a chair to reach the volume of her choice. Naturally, Mother's glasses will help. Will Karen be satisfied with a volume of modest size? Certainly not. The biggest, the heaviest art book, on almost the highest shelf, is what she aims for—a little strenuous, but without outside help she succeeds, as we can see in PHOTOGRAPH 117. No doubt Mother's glasses were of no negligible assistance. She is very pleased with herself, dispensing a broad smile to the adult, out of our visual range, who probably trembled with fear during the climb (the chair does not seem too sturdy or stable a specimen). There is more than just pleasure, rather, a touch of triumph in this broad, expansive smile coming out as she adjusts Mother's glasses on her nose for better vision (incidentally, a familiar gesture of her mother's).

And triumph it is indeed. *All the grownups think you're not big enough, not grown up enough, to do what they do. It's too dangerous. . . . In a few years. . . . Well, just now I CAN look at the art book, and read it. Of course, there are a lot of big words, but I can look at the pictures. Anyway, that's what Daddy and Mommy do. They don't spend too much time on the words. They look at the pictures, like I do. I can see that it's people they look at. People cut in stones. So, what's so hard about that? And if they ask me what do I see? I'll say people, like they do.*

117

21

And some will show talent

Doing easily what others find difficult is talent;
doing what is impossible for talent is genius.

HENRI FRÉDÉRIC AMIEL, *Journal*

With these photographs, we are back at the Goddard Riverside Community School, an integrated school where children ranging from eight to twelve are educated and given opportunities for expression in many fields.

Here, for instance, in PHOTOGRAPHS 118 and 119, is eight-year-old Joey, whose current ambition is to learn music. Music is a word of many meanings, but Joey knows exactly what he wants. Big brother, with a guitar (though not an electric one—it's too expensive), has his group. Four or five of his friends meet once a week at his house for that wonderful sound and noisemaking which big brother calls "rock" (why a rock?). The easiest instrument must be those bongo drums that the big kid pounds on just right. Joey—maybe some day—will play the drums. He is determined now to master the technique.

The teacher has been encouraging and full of patience, but Joey, as he approaches his instrument, suddenly freezes. *The hands of that big kid were moving so fast, and there I am, I can't even move mine.* Intense concentration, watching, listening, but nothing much happens. *My hands are in the right place, but they feel so heavy, so stiff.* Competing with the big brother and his friends may be a

118

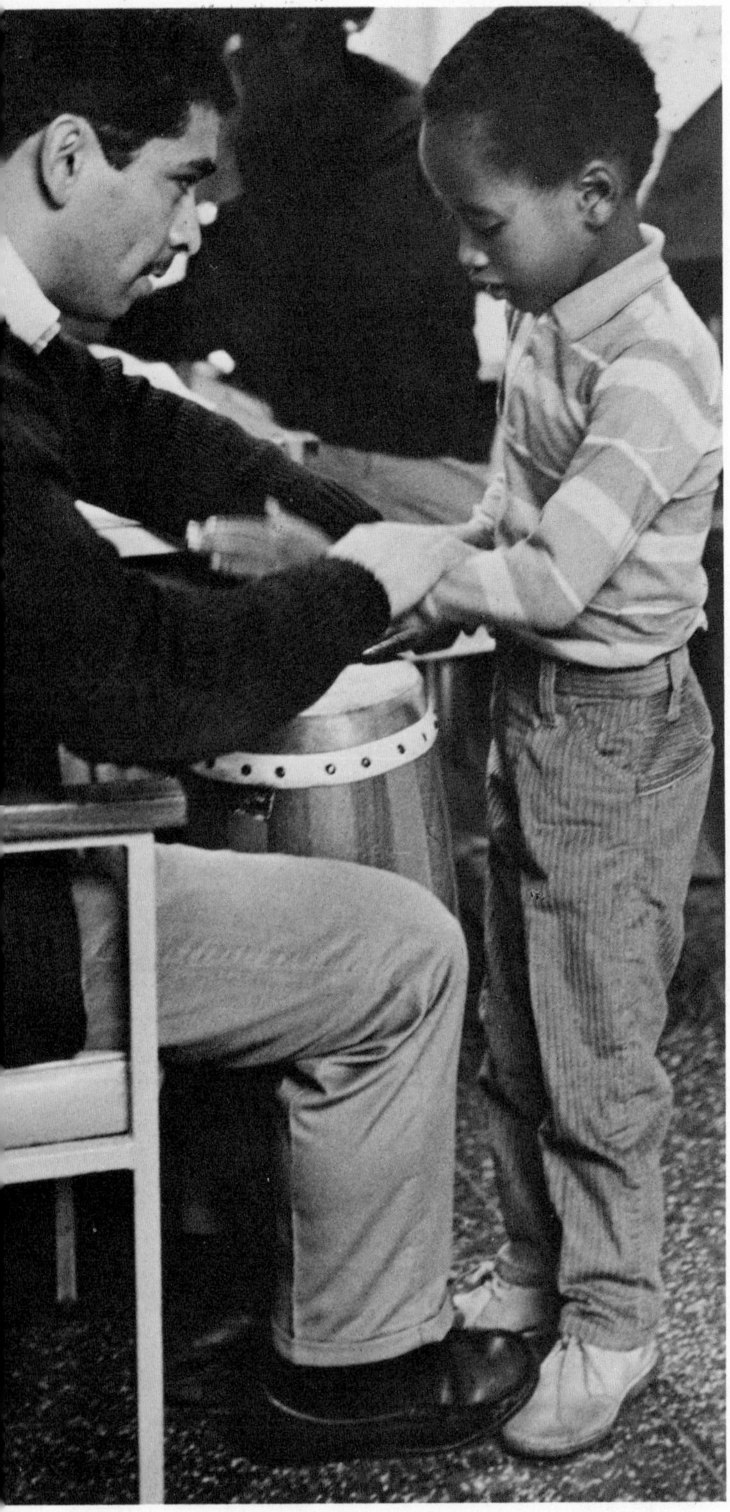

stimulus, but it's also a hardship. After all, did a little kid ever make it like his big brother? Joey is bewildered; his expression is almost painful, with its spasm of anxiety and hopelessness. In PHOTOGRAPH 120 he ends with a defensive gesture as if the drum had suddenly become an enemy.

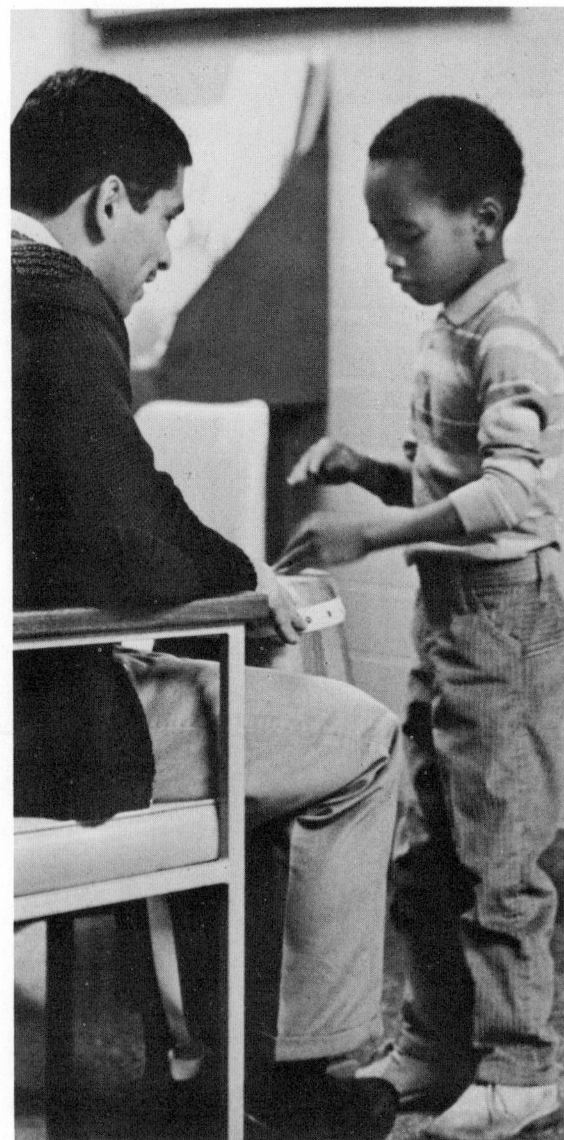

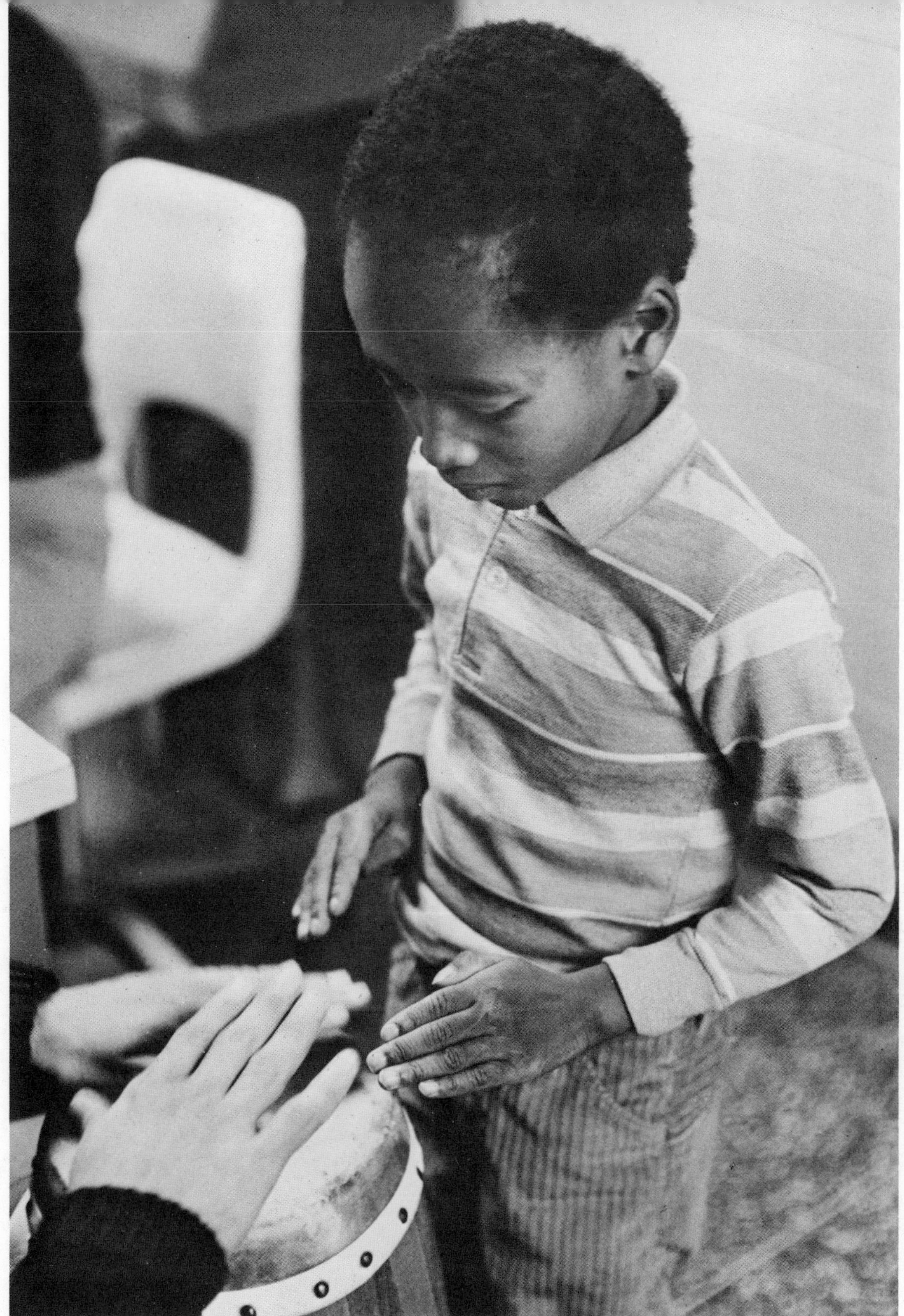

120

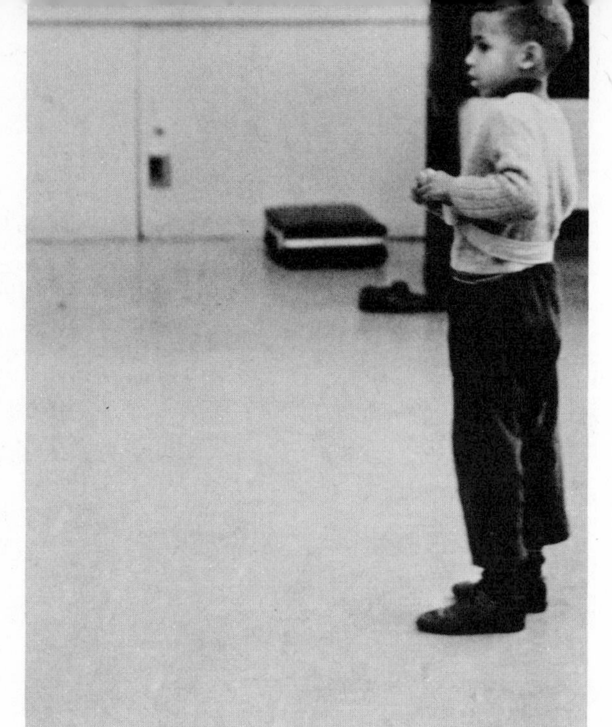

121

In PHOTOGRAPH 121, we have six-year-old Johnny, who is preparing to join the dance group. *Gee! that looks awfully hard. All the kids, they've taken off their street clothes, and look at them. Like real dancers—you show them the step and they do it. Well, maybe if I keep my sweater on, nobody will run after me to make me do those fancy steps.* The time is long past since he took his first steps, walking. He was so small and hesitant before the space ahead, which he felt as immensity without limits. This is the feeling gripping him now—so small, and expected to cover all this ground at a run (he is late) then move arms and legs like a dancer. Johnny has

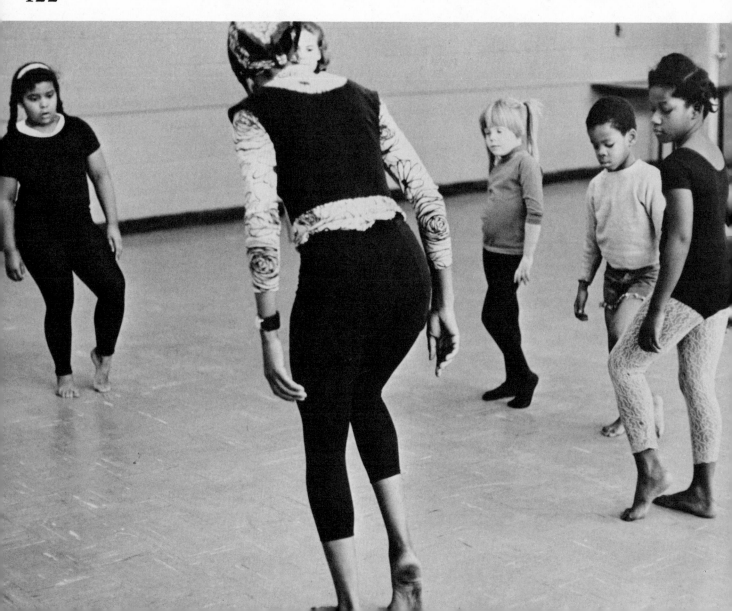

122

124

given up. He will not appear in the next photographs of the dancing group.

The participating children are deeply involved with the teacher's demonstration of techniques. The goodwill and the concentration bring varying results. The lack of familiarity, the inexperience, are reflected in the generally awkward body figurations. The children are attentive, but puzzled. The final outcome is a cross between standing and crouching positions which is exemplified as we follow David, the nine-year-old boy in PHOTOGRAPHS 122, 123, and 124. *All right, the teacher does it so smooth, and so easy. I try, but it's too hard! I bet my behind sticks out*

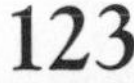
123

more than my foot. It's the leg that won't move right, I know. She don't look at her foot. But how can I know where my foot is if I don't watch it? Funny that the grownups never think of that. They make it fancy, then they say go and do it. That's the same story in school. They forget they had to do it hard at first too. Mom says they have degrees and all that, but they should go back to first and second grades and see if that's so easy. All right, maybe I'll want to be a teacher too when I'm grown up, but there's time.

22

Better not alone

> ... if by chance I were given a sister, would she have been closer to me than Anne Marie [Mother]? Than Karlémami? Then I would have been her lover. Lover was a mysterious word that I often came upon in Corneille's tragedies. Lovers kiss and promise to sleep in the same bed (a strange custom: why not in twin beds, like my mother and me?). I knew nothing more, but beneath the luminous surface of the idea I sensed a hairy mass.
>
> JEAN-PAUL SARTRE, *The Words*

The presence of a baby in its mother's body is the statement of a fact which to the adult seems to require no amplification. To the small child, however, though accepted as a statement, it is at first difficult of comprehension. The fanciful tales of past generations are no longer offered to inquisitive children (the baby picked up at the hospital, or found in strange places), but some parents are still reticent about "the facts of life" despite mass media communications which cannot discriminate between infantile and mature ears.

In fact, young children can be very confused in the face of the two sources of information from which they cull contradictory bits of knowledge. A three-year-old boy, after being told by an older sister where babies come from, saw a very obviously pregnant woman on the street; he said to his mother, "Look at this fat lady. Why is she so fat?" He had been bewildered by his sister's explanation, but now his bewilderment was considably increased when his mother answered, "She probably eats too many potatoes." When queried about this outlandish answer, the mother rationalized that she was not prepared for the child's curiosity, that she was herself very diet-conscious, and, finally, that she thought she would take up the issue at some more opportune time—a time that never came. When the boy developed a severe feeding problem (refusing to eat potatoes at first, then all manner of vegetables), she consulted her pediatrician. His pertinent questioning brought out a correlation between the onset of the child's dislike for food and "the fat lady on the street." At this point, a psychiatrist took over and brought to light a fantasy which had been tormenting the child: he, too, would get a baby if he ate his then favorite french fries. He had quite logically associated "the fat lady," the excessive ingestion of potatoes, and the sister's story about babies being born. All these ostensibly unrelated fragments had spilled out of his unconscious mind. Furthermore, his mother's reticence and fumbling explanation, far from elucidating the mystery of "the fat lady," had given him a sense of what is not talked about, a sense of taboo.

In PHOTOGRAPH 125, we see an eight-months-pregnant young mother with her two children, Jeff, three, and Lisa, four-and-a-half, standing near the shore. Both children know that a little brother or sister is expected, and that the baby is growing in their mother's body, just as they once did, before being born. They have felt its movements, they have put their ears to the abdominal wall, and Jeff is even convinced that the baby whispered something to him. He was not sure *what* was said, but something was said. Children interpret the essence of the birth process at their own level. That words would have been necessary for the transmission of that personal message does not bother Jeff. He perceived a muffled sound, to him it was a whisper, and that's that.

Lisa has completely accepted the arrival of a sibling in the near future, but Jeff is not so sure that this will be a blessing. Indeed, Jeff is not reconciled to the idea of that new baby. As you can see, his mother has a good grip on his arm; not that he cannot be trusted near the water, but of late he has become anxious, somewhat reckless, and she must now keep close watch over him. *That baby, what is it going to be? A boy or a girl, it will make no difference. He will take my place. Mommy can't look after two small ones together. Maybe I could play doll with him. Lisa always says, "Don't touch my Barbie! Boys don't play with dolls." But Ricky holds his baby brother. I saw him. Maybe Mommy will let me hold mine. What if I drop him? Then he would die and I would get punished hard. He wants to be friends with me, that's why he said hello to me. He didn't say anything to Lisa, just me.—All those crazy dreams! Last night I dreamt that my kitten was drowning. But this morning, he was playing with his mother cat. He never wants to go near the water so how could he drown? Just the same, he did.*

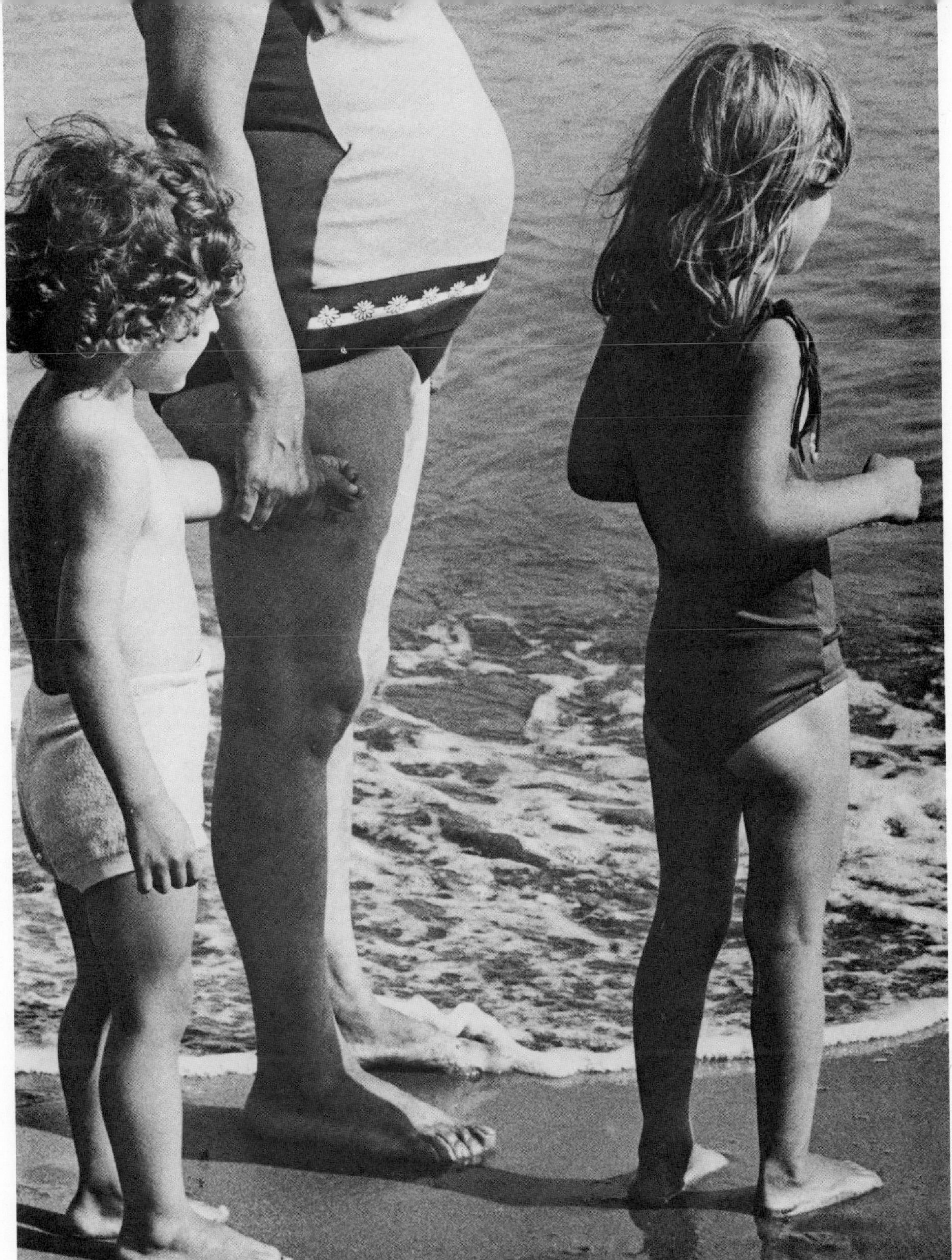

125

23

Brothers and sisters

> My best wishes for this day, may our mutual love increase with the years. I am so glad that we have so many things in common, not only memories of childhood. . . .
>
> VINCENT VAN GOGH, *Dear Theo*
> (Letter to his brother)

We have talked about the disadvantages, from the child's point of view, of being the oldest, or the youngest, or in the middle of a family with two or more children. But there are positive things about this sibling business as well. Between the rivalries and the scrapping, the "He hit me first" and the "You love her better than me," there are many interludes of warmth and sharing, of family fun, of "togetherness"—overworked as that word may have become in recent years.

In PHOTOGRAPHS 126 and 127, three brothers are engaged in a solemn activity. From left to right they are, respectively, eight, six, and five years old; for purposes of convenience, we will identify them as the foreman, the operator, and the onlooker. The operator is celebrating his sixth birthday with a gift specifically his own but which, within a very short time, has become the corporation's property, or at least an object of common interest. The operator is at a loss to start fitting the separate parts, for lack of ability to read the instructions. Only because they are written in fine print, to be sure. So the foreman has taken over, in an attempt to decipher the "how to do it"—a laborious task, demanding complete concentration.

The two younger brothers are in a state of suspended animation, not daring to ask questions, and certainly not making the least suggestion. It has been even harder on the onlooker than on the operator who, from previous experience, counts on big brother to tell him the way to assemble the parts without lifting a finger to "help." The onlooker has shed a tear, furtively dried on his sleeve, such was his frustration at not being allowed to participate. Now, he is all eyes, wanting to absorb everything, even if he is not invited to touch that magic machine. Finally, in PHOTOGRAPH 127, the operator, properly informed about the mechanics involved, starts the joining together of engine and wagons. He could

126

127

not wish for a more attentive audience: the foreman, confident of success, but also watchful; the onlooker intently storing up bits of knowledge that may later come in handy.

The three children are remarkably attuned to each other's needs and wishes. It seems that the inner voices are also attuned. There is a rare quality of oneness, yet each child's personality is clearly differentiated. Their loving and sensible young parents have encouraged sharing of individual possessions. Hostility, aggression, and rivalry have been minimal and their enjoyment of shared toys is quite evident in the photographs.

24

For the control of your body

> Bodily exercise, when compulsory, does no harm to the body. . . .
>
> PLATO, *The Republic*

The imagination of children is stimulated by their new heroes, the astronauts. Especially is this so with boys, who form a strong identification with them. A five-year-old boy in treatment for a severe problem of identity began his male identification in outer space, one might say. Having watched the launching, orbiting, and recovery of rockets and astronauts, he would go through the whole process with accurate and detailed terminology, faithfully reproducing the sound effects and making the props all his own: "My rocket—my launching pad—countdown—blastoff," etc. Does it matter to a young child that a special suit must be worn? One sweeping gesture about his body, and there it is, the suit and even the gait. Does it matter that grownups talk about a rocket as the only thing that can go into outer space? Does it matter that they talk so much about pressure and the dangers of not encugh or too much? If a boy—with himself as the pilot, naturally—wants to go into outer space (that magic word) with a plane, a helicopter, or whatever flies, he can do it. The world—earth, sun, planets with all those exotic names he loves to recite—the world is his own. The mention of a witch can throw him into a panic, but he knows no limit to his adventures in space. There are clouds; he finds "a hole in the clouds" to go out and still farther out. The clouds are in fact the only obstacles he can conjure up since they are the only obstacles he is familiar with. He "drives" his rocket as if it had an automobile wheel, also because of its familiarity.

At the gym of the Goddard Riverside Community School, where exercises in body control are being demonstrated and practiced, a seven-year-old acrobat is not only soaring at a high level, he is off in space. PHOTOGRAPHS 128 and 129 show the group clearly divided into two categories, the actors and the spectators: on the one hand, the instructor and the performing boy, on the other, the three witnesses awaiting their turns but momentarily transfixed before the performance of their classmate in flight. The nine-year-old boy in a striped shirt identifies with the instructor, his left arm crooked at the same angle as that of the adult, his look puzzled by the dynamics of the body support. The two girls at the left

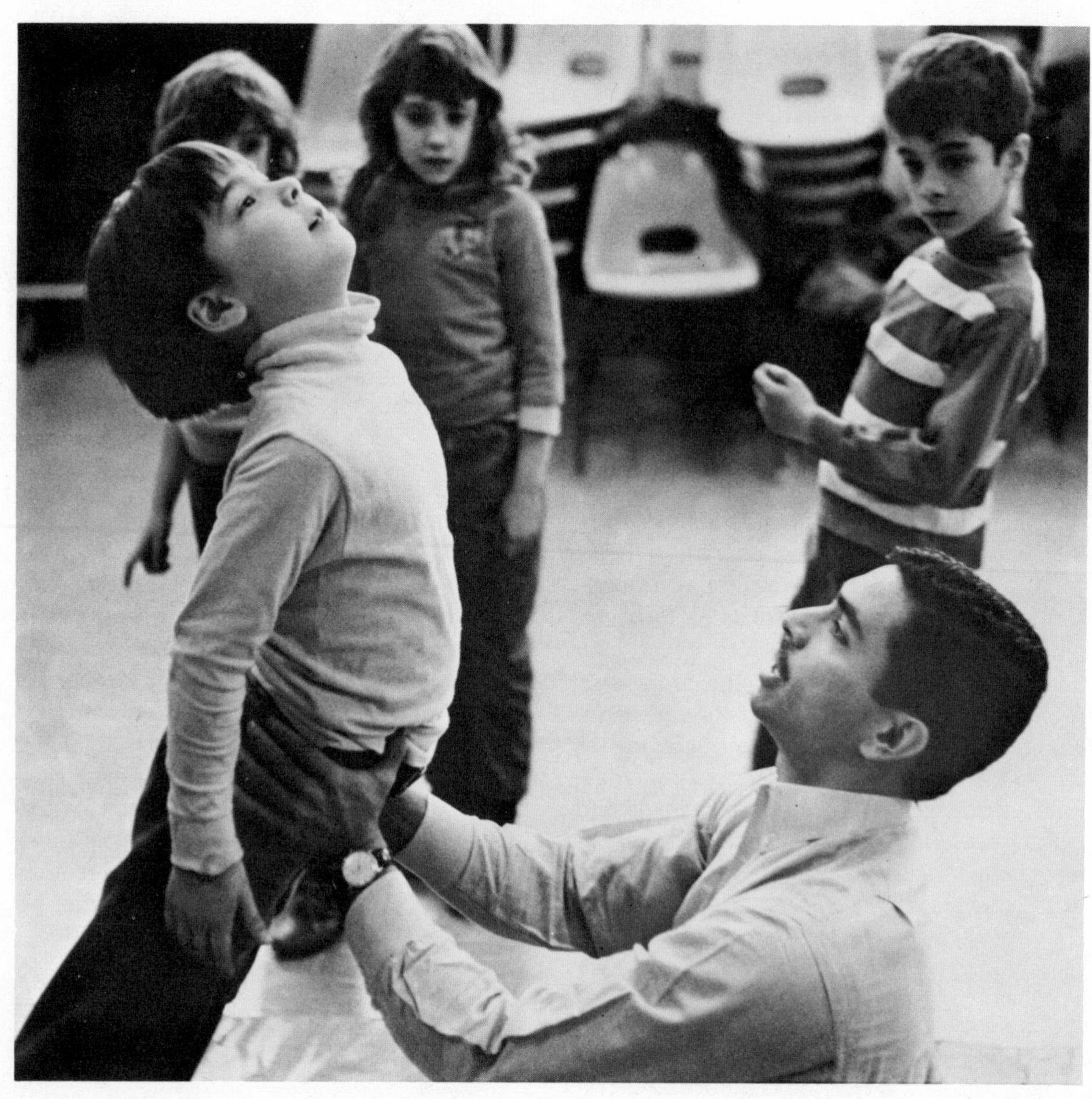

128

are bemused by the boy star, first because he is a boy, and second because he seems able to do some tricks that they do not think they will ever attempt. They will be encouraged by the instructor, but discouragement and hopelessness are registered in advance. *I can run faster, I can jump higher, but try and get so stiff you can be picked up like a piece of wood, no, I can't. How come the boys can do it so easily? Control your muscles—what's that?—in your tummy, your legs, your arms. O.K., maybe it's tougher for girls.*

Our seven-year-old is airborne with no strenuous effort on his part. No driving, no sound effects are necessary. The four grounded children are enormously impressed, but also convinced that, try as they would, they could not make it. One of them crouches on the floor, peering under the elevation, looking for some revealing trick. None is visible. No light is shining in the children's eyes to signal their hope of reaching such heights. Step by step, however, they will learn body control and a few will soar in "outer space."

129

In PHOTOGRAPH 130, we see two boys, seven and six years old, in one of their tumbling routines; two spectators are watching in awe and—in fear (see the revealing gesture of the girl's hands). *Oh, what's going to happen? Sometimes when it's only one in the tumble I'm scared he'll break something. But now the two together—Even if they fit perfect, it's more tough. Denny (the astronaut) knows how to do it, he's good at everything, but look at Michael! I think he's never done it before. He'll crack his head—I shouldn't even look at it, I'm too scared.* The other spectator, a boy, is somewhat intimidated, but he'll take a chance when his turn comes.

130

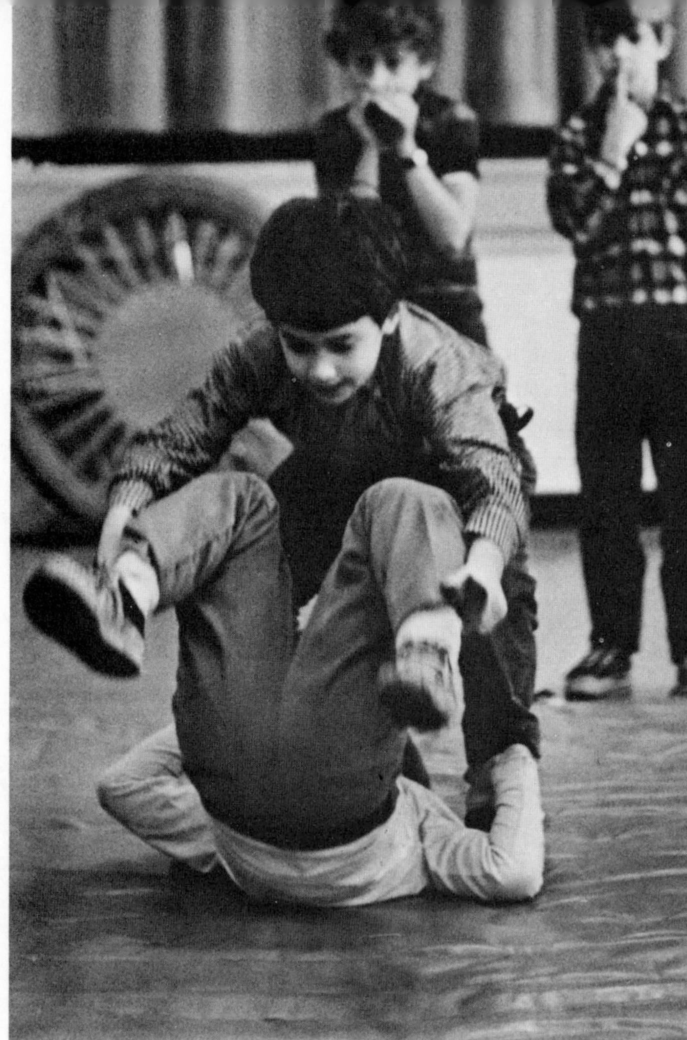

25

No generation gap

The supreme happiness of life is the conviction that we are loved. . . .

VICTOR HUGO, *Les Misérables*

To round off our photographic record, two pictures have been selected for their projection of family intrarelationship: a father and his ten-year-old son, a mother and her two young daughters.

In PHOTOGRAPH 131, Ronnie's father, although currently not feeling his best (he had a heart attack shortly after), has taken his son fishing. This is the boy's first experience as a fisherman. He is a little squeamish about it; while pulling off the hook with one hand, he holds the fish cautiously with the other, a white cloth sparing him from the cold, slimy skin. He gets strong support from his father, who was not at first overly enthusiastic about the boy's request to take part in the fishing trip and yielded only because of his persistence. This is now an operation in which the father seems even more involved than the son. Who is really extracting the hook? *Dad says that's easy, the fish is dead. Funny though—he moves a little bit, how can he be dead? But he can't jump out of my hand. Dad was right when he said that I probably wouldn't like taking the fish off the hook, but he knew I would do it anyway—Gee! maybe he'll get me in his club pretty soon. You have to be a real fisherman like Dad who brings a lot of fish home. Now, I think I'll even like eating the fish. Not right away though. Does some-*

thing to my appetite to see that fish opening and closing his mouth, like he can't breathe. Anyway, I made it. Just like Dad!

PHOTOGRAPH 132 projects a moment of sheer happiness and unity within a small family circle. A young mother is obviously enjoying herself with her five- and four-year-old daughters, the older girl and the mother reacting as one to the babbling of the younger girl, who is seen from the back. This is an interminable story such as only small children can weave, made up of fragments, totally unrelated on the surface, the only link being that it all happened to the storyteller, and that the fragments have the same start: "And . . ." Young children assume that the listener is informed about what has preceded their current account, and that comprehension of things unsaid is total. "And you know what? The grandma said to the fox, 'You have great big eyes.' Maybe that was a wolf. And Celia says it's only pretend but I know, there's a real wolf—I see him at night—and he says grr grr, I get scared—and I don't move—maybe the fox will go away. And Charles took my doll and he made her the mommy, and the mommy spanked all her children." The older sister and the mother listen with great attention and that's what mothers and siblings are for, to listen and to share.

131

132

Postscript

The old Victorian saying, "Children should be seen and not heard," is no longer valid. Children in our society ARE heard. The playgrounds, the children's parties, the adolescents' meetings, and many other manifestations bear witness to the new freedom. Intrafamily communication tends to diminish as the communications mass media multiply, but children still have a voice, and indeed are very much heard.

Is what we hear, however—the sum total or even the most meaningful content of children's verbal expression—a significant projection of their inner life? We know that they learn very early to repress not only actions but also words which they feel would not be approved and could bring a loss of parental love. These repressed thoughts and feelings are the material the psychotherapist deals with, but the discrepancy between inner and outer voices, though smaller than in disturbed children, still exists even in emotionally healthy children.

The children we have seen in the photographs assembled in this volume are free from the emotional problems that lead children to a psychotherapist. They have been photographed at school, in a pediatric (not psychiatric) clinic, in the open air, or in their individual homes. Nevertheless, inner voices can be heard. If a complete chronological range of experiences has not been registered, this is owing to practical obstacles: to be valid, the photographs had to be candid; posed photographs would have defeated our purpose. We hope that our sampling, limited as it stands, represents essential phases of a child's emotional development. Take, for instance, the feeling of smallness and helplessness of the young child, who compensates for this feeling through fantasies of grandiose achievements and identification with adults. Take also the sibling situation, illustrating the conflicts of both the older and younger sibling which must be understood, accepted, and relieved by the parents, whose insight is what makes possible the transition to easier relations between the siblings. Girl-boy attitudes have been fully illustrated, as have the parent-child relationship. Ambivalence of feelings, so characteristic of children, has been projected in explicit images.

It has been seen that words are not necessary for the inner voices to be manifested. When words are first learned and used, there is no guarantee that they will accurately express the thoughts intended. The young child is immersed in a plethora of sounds which are more meaningful through the accompanying affective tone than through phonetic patterns. A four-year-old boy, of superior intelligence, is overheard in his nursery school group formulating his conception of three American presidents: "Day before yesterday will be Lincoln's birthday—George Washington was the father of our country and President Roosevelt has infansis supralsis." To this child, the concept of the three presidents is very definite, even if to the adult mind a few notions are unclear, ill-defined, and even false, time being most flagrantly inaccurate. In the same vein, a three-year-old boy, also bright, having been given a birds-and-bees explanation about conception and birth, goes about his group, his hand cupped over some imaginary content, asking, "Do you want my seeds?"

Words can betray the child's power of expression, but the inner voices hardly need words, although at a later stage of development they utilize this medium. Facial expressions, rapid, tic-like movements about the eyes, the mouth, the nose, give the message without words. Images and feelings spring from the unconscious, which can be further tapped for significant material via projective techniques, or interpretation of symbols in play, dreams, etc., whenever this is investigated for purposes of diagnosis and/or therapy.

The children included here were not "patients," and it was not intended to make an in-depth study of psychodynamics. What is revealed of the inner life in an instant, candid take has been our central interest. Much can thus be observed that the child is unable or unwilling to communicate: a danger signal, or an indication that a behavior is not fully understood and needs sympathetic clarification. A child's behavior is at once simple and complex: simple, because it is spontaneous, free from design or deliberate cover-up; but also complex, because surface emotions do not necessarily correspond to deeper feelings. There is the additional complication of the confrontation between reality and fantasy, which is not as clearly delineated as with the adult; the younger the child, the thinner is the differentiation.

We hope that this book, through its images, will have helped sharpen the curiosity and perceptiveness of those concerned primarily with children—parents, educators, and psychologists.